Witchdom of the True

Witchdom of the True
A Study of the Vana-Troth and the Roots of Seiðr

Second Edition

Edred Thorsson

From a Manuscript formerly entitled
"True-Wicca"

Copyright © 2018
Runestar

All rights reserved. No part of this book, either in part or in whole may be reproduced, transmitted or utilized in any form or by any other means electronic, photographic or mechanical, including photocopying, recording, or by any information storage and retrieval system, without the permission in writing from the Publisher, except for brief quotations embodied in literary, scientific articles and reviews.

For permissions wrote the Publisher at the address below:

Cover art from Olaus Magnus *Historia de gentibus septentrionibus* Book III (1555

Published by:
Runestar
P.O. Box 16
Bastrop, Texas 78602

runa@texas.net

Acknowledgments

I wish to thank Stephen A. McNallen, a long-time leading light of the Ásatrú movement, and Inga, a Wiccan High-Priestess, for their reading of the manuscript. Thanks also go to James Chisholm for his work on the primary materials dealing with *seiðr* and to members of the *Seið*-Network in the Rune-Gild for their continuing Work. I also wish to express my gratitude to Jeff Grandmason for his work on the maps in this volume.

Abbreviations

ON	Old Norse
BCE	Before the Common Era (= "BC")
CE	Common Era (= "AD")
ch.	chapter
fem.	feminine
Go.	Gothic
masc.	masuline
OE	Old English
O.Ir.	Old Irish
PIE	Proto-Indo-European
sg.	singular
st.	stanza

Note on Orthography

The characters ð and þ are the *edh* and *thorn* respectively and stand for the later combination /th/.

Table of Contents

Acknowledgments...v
Abbreviations..vi
Preface..ix
Introduction...xi
Chapter 1: THE HISTORY OF THE VANIC WAY.........................1
  Vana-Troth..3
    Scandinavia...3
    Germany...4
    England...7
  The Northern Wave..8
  Cradle of the Witchdom of the True..10
  Christianization..12
  Fate of the Gods..13
    The Written Records..13
    The Old Gods in Christian Garb...14
  The Gods as Devils..15
  Folk Survival...18
  Rebirth...19
    The Gardnerian Synthesis...20
Chapter 2: THE WORLDS OF THE VANIR.............................25
  Wanehame..27
  Osyard..27
  Etinhame..27
  Alfhame...27
  Dwarfhame...28
  Middlert..28
  Muspellhame...28
  Niflehame...29
  Hel...29
Chapter 3: GOD-LORE..31
  Theology..31
  Æsir and Vanir..31
    The Lord and the Lady..33
    The Lady: *Freyja*...34
      Freyja's Names..34
      Freyja's Animals..35
      The Worship of Freyja...36
    The Lord: *Freyr*..38
      Freyr's Animals...40
      The Worship of the Lord...41

Nerthus/Njörðr: Mother/Father of the Wanes?........ 42
Other Divinities.. 44
    The Wights.. 44
    Elves... 44
    Dises... 45
    Dwarves... 45
    Etins... 45
Worship of the House-Wights.. 47
Chapter 4: THE MYTHS OF THE VANIR....................... 49
  The Myths of Freyja... 50
    Gullveig-Heiðr... 50
    Freyja and the Brisingamen.. 51
    The Rune of the Brisingamen...................................... 52
    Freyja and Óðr... 53
  The Myths of Freyr.. 54
    Freyr and Gerðr... 54
    The Slaying of Beli.. 55
  The Myths of Njörðr.. 55
    The Myth of Njörðr and Skaði..................................... 55
Chapter 5: CALENDAR OF THE WICCAN
WORKINGS OF THE TRUE.. 59
  The Ritual Formula of Witchdom................................ 65
Chapter 6: *WICCECRÆFT* AND *SEIÐR*:
      The Magical Ways of the Vana-Gods............... 69
  The Historical Relationship
    of *Wiccecræft* and *Seiðr*... 70
  Wiccecræft.. 71
  The Vocabulary of *Seiðr*... 72
  Etymology of the Word *Seiðr*..................................... 74
  Uses of *Seiðr* Reflected in the Historical Record.... 75
Appendix A: Witchcraft and Runecraft:
      Two Different Paths... 83
Appendix B: Ásatrú and Vanatrú.................................. 87
Appendix C: Ásatrú and Modern "Wicca"................... 89
Appendix D: Traditional Witchdom and Modern Wicca 91
Notes... 95
Glossary... 96
Bibliography... 99
Map I: Vanic Deity Sites.. 102
Map II: Heptarchy of the Anglo-Saxon England
    and the Danelaw... 103
Map III: The Cult Sites of Freyja.................................. 104
Map IV: The Cult Sites of Freyr.................................... 105
Map V: The Cult Sites of Njörðr................................... 106

Preface

Wiccecræft— Witchcraft and the worship of the Lord and Lady— these are all concepts of extreme antiquity in the Germanic world. In fact, it is in this world, in the Germanic culture, that these forms have come to life again under these very same names. Yet the roots of the tradition have remained obscure. The reasons for this obscurity are many, and some of them will be explored in this book. But the work you have in your hands is a historical call for the actualization of a living form of the old way of *wiccedôm*— "witchdom." Although it contains much that is of a historical nature, it is not meant as simply and a purely historical study. It is meant rather to excite in the reader the possibilities of a return to the true "wicca"— the *wiccecræft* of our ancestors and to a new loyalty to our Gods and hence to theirs.

People who have long been initiates of what has come to be called by some the "craft," or those who have perhaps never before considered it for one reason or another, will find the contents of this book useful— and it is hoped, enlightening. As a tradition within the "craft," it presents a new and fresh approach to things by actually taking the radical step of returning to the as yet virtually unexplored roots of the tradition.

The "Old Religion" has been revivified throughout the world in the form of witchcraft for over fifty years now. The centers of the revival of the Old Religion, or Religions, has undeniably been in the Germanic areas of the world— in England (and its colonies), North America, Germany, and even Scandinavia. It is no accident that this is the case. These cultures were among the last to be Christianized and among the first to question the theological and political power of Christianity— reform it, and now begin to overthrow its worn-out ways, and its religious forms that never seemed quite right for us.

When some in the Ásatrú world heard I was writing a book on "wicca" they recoiled and reacted in a shocked manner: "He's writing a book on *what?!*" Followers of "wicca" and Ásatrú, as rivals in the heathen sub-culture, continue to manifest a good deal of friction between themselves. It is my contention that this present-day friction is actually a reflection of the old tension between the Vanic and Æsiric branches of the old way. The friction can only be turned into a beneficial flame if it is understood for what it is— so that all involved can see clearly the world in which they find themselves and also see how that world can be made better. (See Appendix C.)

In some ways this book might be called *an anti-wiccan treatise* if one understands "Wicca" to mean the neo-pagan, eclectic/multicultural, politically correct, eco-Marxist hodge-podge-religion which has emerged from the occult mill of the latter part of the 20th century. But the word *wicca* itself is a Germanic word— and one which reflects a very specific culture. This word, like so much else of our true heritage, has been stolen and twisted into something to serve the interests of the established cultural authorities. The present book is concerned with wresting this part of our heritage back from the new occult establishment.

One of the main areas of interest in the program of publications at Rûna-Raven Press has been the presentation of various forms of Germanic spirituality to a wider readership. We have also endeavored at all times to present the most accurate and authentic material possible. This work is yet another in this series, and we trust it will fulfill its mission of expanding the horizons of the existing Wiccan movement, while at the same time give a Wiccan (or Vanic) option to those who are *true* to the old Gods and Goddesses of the ancient North.

When we say "true" we mean it in the sense of being *loyal*. The *true* religion is the one in which one maintains age-old loyalties of blood and ancestry. We are *true* to our Gods and Goddesses as we might be *true* to our families or lovers— for are the Gods and Goddesses not our ultimate families and our ultimate lovers?

But as with all "new religions," even ones that harken back to very ancient roots, there are growing pains. There are times of simple enthusiastic beginnings— growing into more and more self-conscious and self-aware levels of being. In the case of the "Old Religion" part of this process will be the seeking and finding of its actual roots and the activation of the power of those roots through an operative harmonizing of the ancient forms with new forms. As this harmonizing gives rise to a new song, its call will be that which can open the gates to a new beginning— when we will again discover in the grass the golden tokens of the Gods.

Edred
Woodharrow
Jóltíð, 1998

Introduction

In the ancient North a race of Gods and Goddesses, called by the Scandinavians the Vanir, was worshipped. Central to their theology was the worship of the Lord and Lady, called in their language *Freyr* and *Freyja*. The "magic," or operative spiritual technology, practiced by these divinities, especially the Lady (Freyja) was called *seiðr*. This magical technology was probably closely related to, if not virtually identical with, that known in the Old English or Anglo-Saxon world as *wiccecræft*.

Indeed, the root of the (modern) word "*wicca*" is Anglo-Saxon— or, if you will, English. It stands to reason that some of the important roots of the ideas and practices signified by the word are also to be found in the culture and history of the English. Not only are its distant roots there— but when the time came for the tradition to be reborn, it was on English soil that this rebirth took place.

Several writers on modern Witchcraft have noted the fact that the word *wicca* is of English or Germanic (and *not* Celtic) origin. This fact is uncontested among scientific scholars. But it appears to be difficult for many to make any far-reaching conclusions based on this, or to allow that overriding cultural fact to open new (and old) doors for exploration. This has largely been due perhaps to the general Celtophilic basis of neo-paganism in England (mainly among *English* writers), coupled with an equally general Germanophobic bias in those same circles. The purpose of this book is to open those doors and to explore what lies beyond them.

This book is called the Witchdom of the True because it is based on the idea that the Lord and the Lady, the God and the Goddess of the *wiccan*, must have been deities of a certain number of the Saxons, Angles, and Jutes who began settling in Britain in the 5th century CE— the wiccan of today may also be *true* (loyal) to those very same *ancestral* deities. The use of the word "true" does not necessarily mean or imply that other forms of modern "Wicca" are not valid or real— the "true" of which we speak is a matter of *loyalty* to the original and ancestrally inherited God-forms which embodied the system as it was used by the ancient Anglo-Saxons around 1500 years ago.

The word "*wicca*" never signified the institution or practice of "witch-craft." A *wicca* [WITCHah] is a male practitioner of *wiccedôm* (witchdom), *wiccecræft* (witchcraft), *wiccung* (witching). A *wicce* [WITCHuh] is a female practitioner of those same skills.

In the modern revival of Witchcraft there seems to have sometimes been unclear tensions between the magical *practices* implied by witchcraft and the *religion* centered around the worship of the Lord and Lady. (For example the annals of historical witchcraft are full of accounts of witches who have the power to curse their enemies to death, but this sometimes hardly seems to jibe with the gentle precepts of an Earth-centered faith.) A return to the ancient roots clarifies these tensions— and heals them.

Of course, witchcraft is surrounded by a recent body of historical facts. The synthesis of traditions provided by Gerald B. Gardner was an important one in the history of the revival of the way of the Lord and Lady. It is a bringing together of Masonic ritual, what was known from folklore and "witch-hunting" literature about medieval and Reformation Age witchcraft, ceremonial magic, and the folklore of the British Isles as gleaned from the works of Margaret Murray and later Robert Graves, along with ideas and rituals picked up from the Woodcraft movement of early 20th century England. Part of this synthesis was probably blended on a conscious level— but some things must have seemed to come directly out of the unconscious parts of Gardner and some of those around him.

Following the repeal of the British Witchcraft Act in 1951 there was a good deal of publicity, much of it negative, was generated surrounding the activities of Gardner and his witches. The early Wiccans of the 1950s and 1960s took advantage of the tabloids for their own purposes. Although those of a more traditional temperament were outraged, the publicity probably did make the widespread revival possible. Subsequently "Wicca" has grown into a many facetted movement with hundreds of thousands of individuals following its way.

This Gardnerian synthesis provided the basis for the modern cult of "Wicca," although many modern practitioners seem sometimes ignorant of this. Over the years, however, the cult developed in ways he could not have foreseen. In many ways it seems to have become an institutionalized form of occult solipsism. Now there are "Egyptian Wiccans," "Celtic Wiccans," "Sumerian Wiccans," and even "Klingon Wiccans." This subjectivism is not entirely foreign to the essence of old traditional witchcraft. However, in ancient times there was also an objective center to the system, rooted in nature and in the very blood of one's ancestors. Some of the movements which gave rise to Gardnerian witchcraft seem to have understood this clearly. It is to this root and spring of tradition this book seeks to return.

Traditional witchcraft is a description of a set of techniques or practices used for a wide variety of purposes— from religion to magic, from herbalism to sooth-saying. Witchcraft contains a very special set of techniques used mainly by the worshipers of the ancient Germanic deities usually known only by their titles— the Lord and the Lady. These deities belong to a family of divinities known as the *Vanir*— or Wanes. Their roots go right back to the most ancient levels of Indo-European society, culture, religion and magic. Witchcraft is, strictly speaking, a set of practical techniques; the Vana-Troth, or the Way of the Wanes, is the religious context in which these techniques are usually practiced.

It is one of those ironic facts of history that what "should have been" obvious from the beginning has been so thoroughly *hidden* from view for so long. The deep roots were hidden, not by a lack of evidence or some willful conspiracy to conceal them, but by the prejudices and unconscious assumptions of the explorers themselves. The Lord and Lady have infinite patience it seems. But in this *hiding* and in this concealment there has been gestation— there has been growth. The time of a full rebirth is at hand.

Vana-Troth or the true *wiccedôm* (witchdom) was founded in a spirit of radical diversity. Witchdom can be understood within the more all-encompassing movement known variously as the Troth, *Ásatrú* or Odinism. But there will be true rings inside witchdom having no official link with any organization. And so it usually goes with *organic* movements. It has been found that *organic* movements are very difficult to *organize* in any artificial or conventional way. This is perhaps because there are certain laws of nature at work giving such movements shape and form.

In the pages that follow we hope to be able to open doors to the most ancient and culturally authentic and consistent of all Wiccan traditions. For the first time in the tradition explanations of the roots of the Lord/Lady formula and an important component of the meaning of Witchdom can be clearly laid out in ways more consistent with what is known of cultural and religious history. The Craft of the Witches will truly be reborn, the Way of the Wanes will truly be known.

Addendum to the Introduction 2018

This edition is a reprint of the Rûna-Raven edition of 1999. This project was originally intended to be the beginning of a larger and more extensive one in which the rituals and other customs of the Vana-Troth, or Vanatrú, would be developed and published. That is why the original volume was characterized as "Volume I." As it stands this more extensive project is going to have to be undertaken by others, if at all. What the present volume indicates is the basics of what we know of the Vana-Troth in a historical and philosophical sense. It remains a thesis of the book that the practices in the Anglo-Saxon world which came to be indicated by the terms connected to Old English *wiccecræft* are part and parcel of practices linked with the practice of the lost ritual and customary technology of the gods and goddesses known in Scandinavia as the Vanir.

The only practical off-shoot of this experiment has been the publication of the now rare little volume *Wiccan Sex-Magic*. We hope to publish this again in an anthology in 2020.

In a sense, we can only know those parts of the ancient Vana-Troth which have been recorded, either in written documents or etched into the behavioral fabric of the folk, and in both cases this must have survived to the present day. However, there may be a more mysterious avenue to access information about the elder gods and goddesses by retrieving material from our own collective unconscious. If this contains archetypes inherited from our ancestors — encoded most logically within our DNA or some mysterious analog to it — then they should be accessible to us directly using certain spiritual or psychological techniques. A useful work in this regard is Alice Karlsdottiir's *Norse Goddess Magic* (Destiny, 2015).

The mission of this book is now what it was in 1999— to form a foundation for the development of an authentic Vanic reawakening based on the best sources and methods at our disposal. I welcome questions and comments

Chapter 1

THE HISTORY OF THE VANIC WAY

The Way of the Wanes — craft of the true — is unbounded by time or place. The wiccan way and the Vanic path were things in essence and structure brought along with the great Indo-European horde as it streamed, and sometimes trickled, out of central Asia beginning about 4000 BCE. These Indo-Europeans, or Aryans as they call themselves in the East, had fully settled in northern Europe by 2000 BCE. With them they brought their language and their divinities along with the mythologies shaped by those Gods and Goddesses.

Recent theories expressed by scholars such as Colin Renfrew would even suggest that the Indo-European culture had its ultimate origins in Europe, along the Danube as early as 6000 BCE, and that a group of them had left the original homeland, took up the horse-riding and more war-like ways of the steppes, and subsequently re-invaded the European homeland. Others, such as Marija Gimbutas, maintain that the Indo-Europeans had a culture fundamentally unlike that of the Old Europeans who are seen as a Goddess-worshipping, peaceful people.

In any event the Indo-European cultural model and languages would eventually shape the cultures of the Germanics, Celts, Slavs, Italics, Hellenics (Greeks), Iranians (Persians), Indians and a other less well-known groups. In each area the incoming "Aryans" certainly intermarried with the already existing populations of Old Europe (many of them perhaps also Indo-European) and often cultures and religions were to some extent blended. In any event most cultures in Europe were rapidly almost totally Indo-Europeanized. We know almost nothing of the languages, cultures, and religions of any supposed "pre-Indo-European" inhabitants of Europe.

If Renfrew is correct it may well be so that most of the "native inhabitants" of Europe when the invaders from the east arrived were in fact also originally Indo-European themselves. This would help account for the relatively easy time the invaders had in the central and northern parts of Europe in establishing their culture. Regardless of whether Renfrew is correct, the thorough Indo-Europeanization of the "Old

Europeans" is a testimony not so much to the military superiority of the invaders (which they had) as it is to the great *prestige* which they enjoyed.

The religious pantheon of the Indo-Europeans mirrors their idealized social structures. (This is explored more in-depth in chapter 3.) One part of that timeless social structure— the form of the relationships between and among the Gods themselves — is a polarized, or dualistic aspect. This is sometimes envisioned as young male twins (for example among the Greeks as the *Dioskures*), sometimes in equine form (for example in India as the *Ashvinaus*). But among the ancient Germanic folk this function was most pointedly represented by the divine twins, brother and sister, who were usually known by their titles: the Lord and the Lady (Old Norse: Freyr and Freyja).

These divinities were brought along to Europe by the Indo-European invaders. There were probably similar deities already living among the "Old Europeans"— but little to nothing survived of their cults. We do not know what the names of any "pre-Indo-European" divinities might have been, what myths might have surrounded them, or by what rites they were worshiped. So it is important to remember and realize that the paradigm of the "Lord and Lady" is an Indo-European model.

The invading Indo-Europeans had a pluralistic, polytheistic culture and religion. There were many Gods and Goddesses and individuals or clans were often devoted to one or a combination of several of these divinities. Among the Germanic peoples the Vanic divinities were especially honored among those folk who cultivated crops (farmers), who worked in the crafts (smiths, woodworkers, cartwrights, and so forth), and musicians and entertainers of all sorts. Among these folk the Vanir — the Lord and the Lady — were supreme. There were other Gods and Goddesses and entities— some very powerful indeed. But none more important to them in their daily lives than the Lord and Lady. These and others of their divine kin provided all they needed— or inspiration, godly gifts, and magic.

Some older scholars (such as Margaret Murray) or other writers on this topic would have you believe that "witchcraft" somehow represents a culture suppressed by the incoming Indo-Europeans. These scholars contend that the "establishment Aryans" subjugated the indigenous population— which went underground (sometimes literally) to practice their "old ways" until they came back to the surface in the middle of the 20th century in England. All of this is highly unlikely in the case of the Lord and Lady. First of all, the mythological or religious pattern is itself an Indo-European or "Aryan" one, if you will— for which there is no evidence among the pre-Indo-European folk. Its terminology and mythology are all purely Indo-European.

Besides this, to believe that the "Gods of the Witches" belonged to a historically and culturally "inferior" and "backward" people is to condemn them (in some people's eyes) to historical irrelevance. To posit a historically evolutionary model for this process is to say — as James Frazer did — that the older more "savage" divinities are overcome by a more "civilized" God, which was to say, Jesus Christ— who in turn is to be overthrown by the One-True-God: *Science*. This is Frazer's evolutionary theory— highly influenced by the Darwinism of the day. It is rather dismaying to see today how many would-be Neo-Pagans hang on Frazer's theories and believe in his models and many of his conclusions concerning the mythologies of the vegetative cycles, dying Gods, Divine Kings and so forth— when his whole theory was one originally constructed to show how *primitive* and "savage" such things were when compared to the true religion of Christianity, and in turn how quaint the Christian theology was when compared to Science. This is typical *modern* thinking. But we now live in a distinctly *post-modern* world. Frazer himself, with his evolutionary theories, has been superseded in the halls of academia. But the legacy of his theories is still alive— because it is so widely available to the public.

The true way of the Wanes is not bound by history. The Vanir are not forgotten deities of a half-forgotten people. They were always with us, are with us now, and shall be with us through eternity as long as the soul of our folk exists. To reduce the Vanir to *historical models* (no matter how Romantic the intention) is to reduce a part of the folk-soul to a historical phenomenon. The Vanir — like all the Gods and Goddesses — are eternal and timeless. They are as alive today as they were 2000 years ago— it is we who have merely lost our *awareness* of their reality.

Vana-Troth

Scandinavia

The Wanes and kindred Gods and Goddesses were known in ancient times among all the Germanic folk groups. As we have learned the complex cult was brought to northern Europe with the Indo-European invasions of as early as 3500 BCE. During the first millennium BCE various Germanic groups began to differentiate and to spread out from an epicenter somewhere in present-day Denmark, southern Sweden and northern Germany.

The Scandinavian cult of the Vanir was probably the strongest historical example of the Vana-Troth (ON *Vanatrú*), of the religion of the Vanir. Later we will see how the Scandinavian forms greatly further influenced English traditions.

From the Scandinavian evidence — which preserves the Germanic pagan heritage more intact than any other — we see how the ancients thought of there being two "races" or families of divinities— the Vanir and the Æsir. Among the Vanir the two most important deities are Freyr and Freyja: the Lord and the Lady.

As a side note it is worth mentioning that the Æsir — Gods such as Týr, Óðinn and Þórr — were more the Gods of the aristocracy and the military elite. (This is not to say that at least *some* kings, especially in Sweden, did not derive their authority to rule from the Vanic deities!) The sovereign power, the power to rule, can be centered anywhere— in the judicial, magical, military or economic realms. In modern times we have seen an increasing focus of sovereign power in the military and economic realms of society, and this was certainly not unknown to our ancestors.

Whole regions of Scandinavia were certainly dominated by Vanic culture. Map I shows the areas of Scandinavia in which clusters of temples, groves and other sacred sites dedicated to Vanic deities are to be found. We will indicate similar maps for the individual Vanic Gods and Goddesses in chapter 3.

It is very important to keep in mind that in the Scandinavian ideology of the Vanir, although all three major divinities — Freyr, Freyja and Njörðr — are all important, it is the Goddess Freyja who seems most powerful everywhere.

In general throughout Scandinavia it is clear that the Vanir and Æsir had become highly "integrated" theologically. Although the two "races" of divinities were clearly understood in their unique roles and aspects, this did not lead to widespread religious sectarianism. Many great temples were dedicated to both Æsiric and Vanic deities. The temple at Uppsala, for example, had great statues of Freyr, Þórr and Óðinn. (Note the representation of all three "Dumézilian functions," which will be discussed later) Every region and locality certainly had its own special mixture of divinities.

Germany

In the southern Germanic territory, or "Germany" proper, there is strong evidence for Vanic deities from an early time. Of special interest to us, would be the extreme northern part of "the Germanies"— the areas from which the Angles, Saxons and Jutes migrated to Britain around 450 CE eventually to shape England.

The Roman historian Tacitus, writing in his own description of the Germans during the last decade of the first century CE, reports that the Germans thought of themselves as being divided into three groups, which he calls Ingaevones, Istaevones and Herminones.

Scholars interpret these words as meaning: Ingaevones = Sons of Ingwaz (= the Earth God), Istaevones = Sons of Istraz (= the Honored God), and Herminones (really Erminones, as the Romans constantly added an initial H- to certain Germanic words) = Sons of Erminaz (= the Great God). Again we see the "Dumézilian functions" at work. So it may be that the tripartite division was as much a description of how the tribes were organized internally as it was a description of the divisions among the tribes. It is also true that in traditional cultures — ones that have maintained an internally coherent and authentic understanding of themselves — tribes are often thought of as specializing in different areas of life. It is therefore *possible* that the Ingaevones were originally devoted to the Earth-God.

This idea is borne out by another report in the *Germania* of Tacitus. In chapter 40 he reports that a certain group of Ingaevonic tribes, among them the Anglii (ancestors of the Angles) worshipped a Goddess by the name Nerthus:

> ...they worship in common Nerthus, or Mother Earth, and they believe she intervenes in the affairs of humans, and rides in a procession among the people. On an island in the ocean is a holy grove (*castum nemus*), and in it a consecrated wagon covered with a cloth; a single priest is allowed to touch it. He senses the presence of the goddess in her shrine and reverently follows as she rides away pulled by female bovines. Then come days of celebration, everywhere there are festival days, as many as are thought worthy to receive and entertain her. They make no war, do not take up arms, all weapons are stored away, peace and quiet are known only then, are loved only then, until the same priest returns the goddess to her temple (*templum*) when she has had enough of her interactions with humans. Afterward the wagon and the cloths and, if you want to believe it, the deity (*numen*) itself are washed in a hidden (*secretum*) lake. Slaves carry this out and are immediately swallowed by the same lake. Therefore there is a mysterious terror (*arcanus*

terror) and holy ignorance (*sancta ignorantia*) about that which only those who are doomed to die are allowed to see.

The name Nerthus shows up in Scandinavian sources recorded at a later date as a male God Njörðr — the Vanic father of Freyr and Freyja. The often asked questions about this are: Was Nerthus originally male or female? Did the deity undergo a sexual transformation of historical proportions? On one level these questions are not so important— different regions may have had different traditions. But we will spend some time on this question in chapter 3.

It was from this region in northern Germany and Denmark that the folk who settled in Britain during the 5th century CE came. They surely brought with them some knowledge of their Nerthus-descended deities. (However, it must be pointed out that a great number of the leaders among the invaders were devotees of Wôden— as *every* Anglo-Saxon king traced his ancestry back to the All-Father, Wôden.)

Although not strictly connected with the Scandinavian Vanir, there is also ample evidence for a complex Goddess-cult among the Germans along the Rhine river in the Roman Age. This evidence primarily comes from a great number of votive altar stones, sculptures and inscriptions (in Latin). These are often dedicated to a triad of Goddesses referred to alternately as *Matres* or *Matronae*. The former title seems to refer to the mothers of tribes or whole peoples, while the latter title is used for Goddesses of various other functions. Also among the Rhineland Goddesses is Nehalennia, who is shown riding in a ship, and who may be analogous to Nerthus farther to the North. Nehalennia was mistakenly identified as Isis by the Romans, who were often bad observers of exotic cultures.

The Lombards — or Langobards (Long-Beards) — are an originally northern Germanic tribe which migrated through central Europe into northern Italy (hence the regional name Lombardy) during the late 6th century. In his *Dialogs* (III:28) Pope Gregory I (sometimes called "the Great") tells us that these heathen people (although supposedly already Christianized) would "sacrifice the head of a goat to the devil while dancing in a circle singing terrible songs." This is an extremely important account, as it seems to be a report which already contains the basic elements of the basic magical formula of witchcraft: rhythmic circular dancing motion focused on a (horned) deity. Remember, this account dates from around the year 600 CE— some 800 years before the routine descriptions of supposed "witches' sabbats."

Among the Germans "witches" were known by a variety of terms. In modern German the word for "witch" is *Hexe*. This comes from the Old High German word *hagazussa*. This may literally refer to a woman who was a member of a guild or collegium of seeresses, healers, and sorceresses who lived apart from the rest of society out in rural enclosures which were *hedged-in* places. The first part of the Old High German word, *hag-*, essentially means a hedge or fenced-in enclosure. Even in pagan times these women, because they had power, were sometimes suspected of using their magic in harmful ways. But for the most part they were seen as an indispensable asset to the community. By the way, this word was also known in Old English, where we find *hægtesse*, which eventually developed into our modern English word "hag."

England

Before the middle of the 5th century CE Britain had been dominated by Celtic culture— and since the southern part of the island had been occupied for nearly 400 years by the Romans— the culture of what was to become England was also to some extent Romanized. The Roman occupation had largely eviscerated the cultural, political and religious integrity of the indigenous Celtic population. Christianity had been introduced with some limited success.

The Romans were finally out of Britain once and for all by 410 CE This was largely due to the vast pressures being put on the heartland of the Empire by migrating and invading Germanic tribes on the Continent. When the Romans left Britain they also left a power vacuum in the areas they had occupied. The "Ingaevonic" invaders moved into this cultural and political vacuum.

These Ingaevones — Saxons, Angles and Jutes — brought every aspect of their integral culture with them from their homeland in what is now northern Germany and Denmark. This included their language (Old English), religion (traditional Germanic troth), politics (Germanic sacral kingship and "representative aristocracy").

They did not, however, lay waste to the country-side and migrate *en masse* to Britain from Germany. Although later waves must have brought some of their wives and children with them, for the most part the first invaders were young men who were relatively property-less in their old homeland— they were "going west" as their Indo-European forbears had been doing for centuries and even millennia before. (As we know the movement west did not stop with Britain but continued to America several centuries later— again with westward migrations.)

There was immediate intermarriage with the local (Celtic) Brythonic population. But it is overridingly important to note that the language of the Germanic invaders almost totally subsumed the local Celtic dialect. This is the best and most objective indicator of the degree to which the whole culture was Saxonized. This could also be taken as an indicator of just how much of the continuing authentic heathenry of the English countryside was Anglo-Saxon in origin.

The Germanic tribes eventually set up ten independent regional kingdoms as shown on Map II. Over time these became consolidated to the so-called "Heptarchy" of seven kingdoms. Only with the coming of Christianity did the idea of a strong *monarchy* — one king over all the tribes — arise. Celtic influence was restricted to present-day Wales (*Cymru*), Cornwall, and Scotland. Between the time of the Anglo-Saxon invasions (450) and the second wave from farther north — the Viking invasions — beginning just before 800, the culture of southern Britain (now England) had been thoroughly Germanicized. The Gods and Goddesses of the invaders had been brought — body and soul — to the new land.

There is little doubt that the local Celtic traditions had some influence on the Saxon traditions— for there would have been no real conscious effort to keep Celtic elements out. Besides, the Celts and Germans had had centuries of close cultural contact and often cooperation on the European continent (especially along the Rhine and Danube rivers) as well as across the North Sea. But it must also be kept in mind that the Anglo-Saxons were really only able to conquer and settle and pacify those areas of Britain which had been formerly dominated by Roman culture for about 400 years. These regions were, no doubt, culturally weakened to such an extent that the submerging of what was left of the Celtic culture was not difficult for the vital and vigorous northern waves.

The Northern Wave

In the year 793 the first "Viking raid" was made by Norwegian adventurers/pirates on the monastery at Lindisfarne in northern England. This signaled the beginning of a large cultural movement from still heathen Scandinavia out over the seas to the west — to England, Ireland, Spain, France and even North Africa — and over the rivers and inland seas to the east to Russia, Greece, and even to Persia.

The word "viking" is a much misunderstood and misused term. It comes from Old Norse *víking*, which means a voyage for the purposes of raiding and/or trading to gain wealth and fame. Most typically young men would get longships from their fathers and set out on a voyage. They would raid and trade—

perhaps making several "trips" (usually in the spring and summer) perhaps over several years until they were wealthy enough to establish themselves— either at home in Scandinavia or in colonies abroad. The term "Viking" only really describes one aspect or *activity* within Scandinavian culture between the years of 800 and 1100. But it should also be pointed out that this pattern of activity— bands of young men raiding and trading in foreign regions (some of them eventually conquering and settling there) — is the pattern most responsible for not only the migrations from Germany to England but even the great millennia-long movements of the Indo-European peoples out of the region around the Caspian Sea.

The Scandinavians who raided in the British Isles found England especially to their liking. This was due to the fact that England had maintained close cultural and economic ties with Scandinavia and Anglo-Saxon and Norse were languages very closely related to one another. Especially the Danes found a home there— after all it was from just south of the Danish region that the Angles, or English, had originally come. Even the English "national epic" *Béowulf* is in substance a Danish tale which takes place on a Danish landscape.

So between 800 and the year of the Norman Conquest (1066) the Scandinavian culture had an enormous impact on England and the English language— especially in northern England. The Kingdom of York was a Scandinavian realm first established by the Danes around 865. This northern region is sometimes called the "Danelaw." (See Map II.) By the time of the Norman Conquest, England had become part of a greater North Sea cultural sphere. William the Conqueror's claims to the throne of England had much more to do with Scandinavian affairs than they had to do with purely English politics.

The Norman (Nor[th]man) French were originally Norwegians who in 911 had won a duchy in northern France under their leader Göngu-Hrólfr (Walking-Rolf)- or as he came to be called in French, Rollo. Basically this fiefdom was a way of "buying off" the Viking raiders. Although the Normans became Francicized (they had lost their native Norse tongue by the second generation) many of their cultural features in the areas of the royal cult, military traditions, and political organization remained with them from their Scandinavian heritage.

The Norman French overlay was the last major element to be added to the English cultural mixture, which might best be described as Anglo-Saxon blended with Scandinavian (especially in the north) over a Brythonic substructure— with the whole overlaid with a Franco-Norman veneer. Because the Normans were not "real Frenchmen" the influence of French culture was mixed: on the one hand the linguistic influence was tremendous, and the impact on political theories was disastrous. While the Norman kings were among the greatest warriors in Europe, they had also learned un-Germanic political theories that put the kings in a more tyrannical position over the folk than the English (or any Germanic system) had previously allowed.

But the questions of whether the Germanic Gods and Goddesses ever penetrated to the rural "peasant" level of English society, and if so, how well these Gods survived are pointedly answered by the text of a magical charm recorded in the late 19th century in Lincolnshire:

> Feyther, Son an' Holi Ghoast,
> Neale the devil to this poast.
> Throice I stroikes with holy crook:
> Won for God, an' won for Wod, an' won for Lok.(1)

This shows that the heathen Gods continued to be known at the folk-level right alongside the Christian "Gods." It also shows that the God Lok(i)— who was a purely Scandinavian figure unknown to the Anglo-Saxons before the arrival of the Vikings — was integrated with the Anglo-Saxon pantheon and survived as a part of it. The same was surely true of the Lord and Lady. By the way, there is evidence to show that the "God" referred to in the last line of the charm is not the Christian God, but Thunar (Þórr).

Cradle of the Witchdom of the True

We believe that the craft of the true was given its final inner shape in the period between 800 and 1100 in England. It was in that time and place that three great cultural influences met on the field of ancient neolithic tradition. The Celtic British, the Anglo-Saxons, and the Scandinavians all poured forth their inspiration into the cauldron first brought to a boil by the pre-Celtic neolithic folk of the island. Each of these four groups had something to add to the brew. The neolithic folk lent the subtle, yet powerful, traditions connected with the land itself and the stones they had set in it. The Celtic British (Britons) provided much of the lore and magic of the plants and natural cycles of the land— the link between humans and nature. Even in Old English one word for magic, *drýcræft*, seems to have been borrowed from Celtic, and to be related to the Celtic *druid*, priest. The Anglo-Saxons, who had dominated the land and culture for over 300 years prior to the beginning of the Viking Age, provided the major religious, mythological, and linguistic forms for the tradition. The vocabulary of actual witchcraft (that is excluding that which the Christian witch hunters provided) is almost purely Anglo-Saxon. This modern fact has its roots in the ancient circumstance that English was the dominant cultural force on the island following 450 CE To this Anglo-Celtic mixture, the Norse — who began settling in England just before the middle of the 9th century — added the deciding factor: the well developed cult of the Lord and lady. Freyr and Freyja were largely Norse influences. Also a good deal of the magical and ritual technology was the result of Norse influence. Although the English had mostly become at least nominally Christian by 800, the largely still pagan Scandinavians began to reverse this trend among the English.

It is most likely that if the traditional culture had survived and established a religion in England, that religion would most probably have been a blend of Anglo-Saxon and Norse elements— with a Celtic substratum.

It is perhaps for this reason that the revival has taken a similar direction.

Although *wiccecræft* [witch-uh-craft] as such is a Germanic or Anglo-Saxon form of magical technology and the religious practices associated with the Gods and Goddesses of the agricultural and natural cycles, its roots are actually quite eclectic. From its beginnings it was a kind of tradition open to new influences and forms. This is the source of its strength and viability. In the recent revival of *wiccecræft* the neolithic and Celtic aspects were recognized first. Then some efforts were made to indicate the English or Anglo-Saxon component. But the final element in the composition of true witchdom is that of the Norse. Once it is added the other three components will make more sense than ever.

We recall how close the Norse and Anglo-Saxons were culturally, religiously, linguistically, and how they were even economically closely linked. Their societies were organized in similar ways, they had the same pantheon of high Gods and Goddesses, their languages were descended from the common root of Proto-Germanic (and they could easily learn each other's tongues). At the time in question — from the 8th to the 11th century — the North and Baltic Sea regions really made up a sea-going pan-Germanic economic empire ruled from power centers in Sweden, Denmark and England.

The degree to which the Norse language influenced English can be seen on any page of an English dictionary. You will note how many words are derived from Old Norse originals. Also, words closely shared by Norse and English took on different meanings in English. An example of this is found in the words "shirt" and "skirt." Shirt comes from OE *scyrte* [shewrt-a], meaning "shirt," while skirt comes from Old Norse *skyrta* [skewrt-a], also originally meaning "shirt." But when the English found themselves with (apparently) two different words for the same thing, they made the Scandinavian version stand for a slightly different garment, the "skirt." At one point, many people must have been speaking a mixture of English and Norse— and not really noticing the difference.

At the ruling or sovereign levels of society it was the court-based Æsiric cult of Wôden/Óðinn which was paramount. At the level of the free land-holders it was the cult of Thunar/Þórr which tended to dominate. These tendencies had their local variations depending on religious and cultural balances in different regions.

But at the outer reaches of society where the boundaries between the different folk-groups were most permeable and where the line between the "classes" was most vague— this is where the Vanic way was strongest. It must not be thought that this "line" was a thin or rare one either— it was a great and broad gray swath cutting across the culture, running through all the lands. But it was especially strong in England and in the British Isles generally.

It is worth keeping in mind that the very land where the faith of the Lord and Lady was alive in ancient times — in Anglo-Norse England — is precisely where the revival of their worship was to be found in the early part of the 20th century.

This whole situation is very reminiscent of the way Hinduism and its Tantric schools grew up in the context of the cultural intersection of the Aryan and Dravidian worlds on the Indian subcontinent.

Christianization

The Germanic world was Christianized slowly and in a piece-meal fashion over several centuries. A variety of methods was used by the evangelists— from outright military conquest by monarchal forces with "foreign aid" from the church (as in the case of much of Germany, Norway and Sweden) to slow and superficial political conversion of kings (as in England and Denmark), to the ballot (as in Iceland). The traditional cultural world reacted to Christianity in a variety of ways as well. The two most important reactions came at the two socioeconomic extremes of the cultures in question. The kings accepted Christian priests into their courts and accepted churches in their strongholds—' but at the same time withdrew into a deeper level of royal court culture (with its own lore, customs and ritual) which was largely of heathen origin. The kings were not about to give up their cultural power built up over untold centuries for the sake of a foreign creed— no matter how much money was attached to the deal. This tension would finally erupt in the rise of Protestantism in Germanic Europe during the early 1500s. In *The Cult of Kingship in Anglo-Saxon England* William Chaney gives a brilliant outline of how pagan elements made the transition into the Christian period. But it must be remembered that this court culture is largely Æsiric and Odinic— and not originally particularly Vanic. However, the Lord and Lady were certainly well-known and represented in the court culture of the kings.

At the other end of the socioeconomic spectrum is the mass of farmers, peasants and craftspeople. It was among them that the Lord and Lady felt most at home. (But we should also point out that after the Norman Conquest many, but not all, of the clans and families of the Anglo-Saxon aristocracy were ousted from the high levels of society and "fell" to the level of the "peasantry"— and especially into the crafts.

Among the farmers and craftsmen of medieval England the old Gods and Goddesses survived strongly under Christian disguises and in the form of folk customs. Both kings and peasants were probably equally aware of the vaguely heathen nature of many of their most sacred and revered customs and rituals— and as time went on there was little difference in their minds between the concepts "pagan" and "Christian"— the people had again become just "English." In the 17th century the Puritans of Cromwell were aware enough of many pagan customs attached to the celebration of "Christmas" that most of the traditional practices were actually outlawed during the time they controlled the land.

Fate of the Gods

The elder divinities of the English survived in four different — but often interrelated — ways: there are written records, Christian syncretism (Old Gods become Saints), diabolization (Old Gods become Devils) and folk-level survival in magical practices and country customs. This latter aspect is what is responsible for the remnants of traditional witches in northern Europe.

The Written Records

In many ways the old written records— poems, myths, histories, laws and so forth — from the actual heathen times or in times very close to them are the most *reliable* sources of the tradition. They may be "petrified"— but they are pure, and often lend themselves to rational decoding. These sources also form the most fertile field for the application of magically rational intuition once the basics have been mastered. In the Germanic world the *Poetic* and *Prose Eddas* hold the most interest for those seeking traditional bedrock. But there are actually hundreds of other sources as well. In the realm of Old

English there is the great national epic *Beowulf* along with dozens of other poems. Any deep — or *initiated* — understanding of the tradition must be based on the primary sources themselves— not on secondary interpretations of uninitiated and often unsympathetic scholars and writers of the 19th and 20th centuries. (By the way an honor roll of sympathetic scholars would certainly include Jacob Grimm, Vilhelm Grønbech, Jan de Vries and Georges Dumézil.)

One of the unfortunate aspects of the written record from a Vanic standpoint is that relatively little of this mound of evidence refers to specifically Vanic lore. The lore that tended to survive in written form was — as is always the case — that of the aristocracy, the rulers and the "intelligentsia." That is why there is so much of an Odinic character in the written records. The Vanic lore was more likely to survive in folkways and in "Christianized" forms.

The Vanir did have their myths and poetic lays also. But because of the sometimes overtly sexual nature of a certain kind of them— the *mansöngr* (erotic song) of Freyja were most strictly forbidden and outlawed— even in otherwise tolerant Iceland.

Even with all this there is a great deal we can still learn directly from the old written sources about the way of the Wanes and the true *wiccedôm* [witch-uh-dome].

The Old Gods in Christian Garb

Everywhere Christianity has gone it has had to subsume the worship of native divinities. The mechanism of how this works — or does not work — is very clear when we observe peoples more recently converted to Christianity. Among the Indians and former slaves of the Caribbean and South America — many of whom have only nominally been Christianized for 200 to 300 years. The "creole" systems of religion and magic known variously as *voudon* (in French-speaking Haiti) or as *santería* in Spanish-speaking regions— or similar systems also known as *macumba* (Brazil), *obeah* (Jamaica), and *lucumi* (Cuba) are well known by now. There is really nothing unique about them. The same thing happened in Europe and elsewhere. It is just that the "European Santería" more or less became the establishment (at least externally) after a few hundred years.

Sometimes the pagan divinity or idea was so strong it was itself canonized (made a saint). Good examples are St. Sophia (Wisdom) among the Greeks, or the Irish Goddess Brigid, who was canonized as St. Brigit. But more often the local pagan cultures would find saints who most resembled their own true Gods and Goddesses and would continue to worship them under their Christian *name* and *shape* only. In time the old pagan elements would become so strong they would reshape the stories of the saint's lives. St. George didn't have anything to do with dragon-slaying until his story came to England where this activity was an important part of the initiatory development of the divine hero. St. George had to be "Anglicized" before he could become the "patron saint" of England (and Germany).

Quite often the old divinities were understood to be in the guise of more than one saint. For example Wôden was expressed in different aspects through St. Michael, St. Oswald, St. Nicholas, St. Mauritius, and even in Jesus Christ (as the "hanged" God). Also, single Christian figures might be split up into several pagan deities. For example, Christ is Freyr (as "Prince of Peace" and *Lord*), Baldr (as the martyred one to return at the end of times), and Wôden (as the crucified cosmic God).

Each locality certainly developed its own system of old true Gods and Goddesses in the disguise of saints. The one discovered for Northumbria in England would not likely be the same as the one found in Uppsala in Sweden. But there would be many similarities, to be sure. There can be little doubt that much of the old heathen lore and practice survived in the form of the "cult of the saints."

Some other Vanic correspondences that have been discovered include Freyr in the guise of St. Hubert (patron of hunters, whose symbol is the stag), and Freyja in the guises of St. Lucia (light), St. Walburg (whose day is May Eve), St. Ursula and Mary Magdalene.

A whole study could be developed on the subject of this Germanic or European *"santería"*— but this book is mainly about the direct appreciation of the Vanir themselves— not in Christian garb but in all their naked glory.

The Gods as Devils

"The Devil" of the medieval church was largely a fictional creation hatched in the lurid imaginations of repressed churchmen. Of course, there was no "devil-worship" among the pre-Christian heathens of the north, but the church insisted on the doctrine that anything not of God, must be of the Devil. Therefore aspects of the old Gods and Goddesses were often turned into devils in the legends of the church.

It is well known and well documented that the early church "diabolized" many of the native Gods and Goddesses of local populations as they converted them to Christianity. Given the monotheistic theoretical basis of the faith this was not an altogether unexpected attitude. The heathen deities could not be wiped away overnight— and in fact were never fully eradicated. Actually the lore, myths, rituals and beliefs of the church often accommodated themselves to heathen practices. Examples of this are found in everything from the adoptions of the pagan calendar of festivals to popular things such as the Christmas tree, Santa Claus and the Easter Bunny. Indeed, heathen forms and practices survived in syncretization with Christian customs both positive and negative. As we have seen the old ways were canonized or sanctified in some aspects and diabolized in others.

A fascinating document which shows both that pagan practices continued after nominal Christianization, and that such practices were considered offences by the church is the *Indiculus superstitionum et paganiarum* (Index of superstitions and pagan practices). It dates from early medieval Germany (740 CE). The list represents customs still being practiced in northcentral Europe at the time the *Index* was published. The list reads:

1. On the sacrilege at graves and of the dead.
2. On the sacrilege among the buried dead.
3. On the purification festivals in February.
4. On the little houses, i.e. enclosures for the gods.
5. On sacrileges performed in churches.
6. On holy places in the woods, which are called Nimidas.
    (*Nemeton* = Celtic word for sacred enclosure)
7. On the practices which they carry out on top of rocks.
8. On services to Mercury (= Wōden) and Jupiter (= Þūnor)
9. On sacrifices, which are given to a saint.
10. On amulets and magical bands.
11. On sacrifices at wells.
12. On magical incantations.
13 On auguries by means of birds or horses or from the manure of oxen or from their kidneys.
14. On divination or sortilege.
15. On fire produced by friction from wood, i.e. the Need-fire.
16. On the brains of animals.
17. On the heathen observations of the hearth-fire, or the ignition of these things.
18. On uncertain places, which they hold sacred.
19. On the bundle of straw, which the common folk call St. Mary.
20. On the festivals, which they give to Jupiter (= Þūnor) or Mercury (= Wōden)
21. On the waning of the moon, which they call *Vince Luna*.
22. On tempests and horns and spoons.
23. On the furrows around the yards.

24. On the heathen meeting called *Irias* with torn clothes and shoes.
25. On the belief that they consider every dead person a saint.
26. On idols made from dough.
27. On idols made from cloth.
28. On idols which they carry across fields.
29. On wooden feet or hands according to heathen practice.
30. On the opinion that the hearts of people can be taken away according to the heathens, as women conjure the moon.

This document shows the nature and scope of continuing heathen practice. None of it is particularly "diabolical" — at least not by modern standards — but the official attitude of the church toward such practices was that they were inspired "by the Devil."

In fact the old heathen divinities are many sided, complex entities. Now there is no need, nor was there any in ancient times, to maintain dogmatically that they are wholly "good" unmixed with "bad." Also, of course, some things which are by any healthy yardstick *good* things are considered to be innately evil by Christians— this is why Freyja was so singled out for special persecutions. Just as it is very common for the old deities to take up residence in the guise of saints, certain aspects of them were also driven into the guise of devils or demons. To the basically *pagan* mind saints and devils were just convenient images for the living essences of their true divinities and they probably paid little attention to the strict Christian good *versus* evil dichotomy. (This innocent attitude will lead to some naive "confessions" by accused witches that they "worship the devil.")

Learned churchmen dogmatically condemned all of the old Gods to the level of demons or devils— this was just "standard operating procedure" for the church. This may be part of the reason why the Gods began to be assimilated to saints. It was the only way *back* into the "church" (which had invariably been built on the holy ground of a true sanctuary to the old divinities). But because of the continuing and universal rhetoric coming from the church which condemned the old Gods as devils and demons, some of the more radically stubborn heathens began to see themselves as worshipping "the devil"— at least as the church had defined it. After all the "devil" was usually depicted in Christian art and written descriptions in such a way that made him similar to the Vanic Horned God (in Greece as the satyr-form Pan— complete with cloven hooves, or in England as Robin, or Jack, or Old Nick. Conversely, the "good God" was also depicted in essentially pagan terms— as we see Jesus in the northern climes as the pure image of the wise and bold Tyric king (*long* blond hair with beard). Long hair was a sign of nobility and freedom to the ancient Teutons.

When in medieval times witches confessed to "worshipping the devil" it seems likely that where this was honestly offered (not under torture) it would be a case of the local population merely accepting the church's interpretation that *the old Gods are devils*— and then going ahead and being a heathen *anyway*. To them, we are sure, Old Nick was truly representing aspects of the old Gods just as the saints did for others. But it was probably just as often the case that individual witches worshipped both "saints" and "devils" when it suited them. This was the only way to recover their holistic vision of the heathen past.

It must be remembered that where there had formerly been well trained and established traditional priests, priestesses, skalds and soothsayers there were now only scattered and disenfranchised individuals and small groups desperately, but only half consciously, trying to hold onto what they could of their heritage. Under these conditions — coupled with continued violent programs of repression of "heretics" of all sorts — it is no wonder that the philosophical or theological purity of the folk-way practices began to deteriorate over time. Soon those who had inherited their knowledge in family traditions were probably only vaguely aware of the "pre-Christian" origins of their ways. If they had remained *fully* aware of what they were doing it is unlikely they would have been able to survive the Inquisitions and witch hunts.

Folk Survival

It is perhaps true that at least some of the old Vanic ways were able to survive — at least to the middle of the 20th century — at the level of common rural folk traditions. This seems true for England and northern Europe, as well as for North America. But it is most reasonable to assume that there was a steady decline in the level of traditional witchdom and Vanic customs from the time of the Norman Conquest down to the revival of witchdom in the in England during the first part of the 20th century. Traditional English witchdom did not die out suddenly— in fact it would be a mistake to say that it completely died out at all.

The true *wiccedôm*, as we have seen, is a part of the old cult of the Lord and Lady. Its rituals and terminology are firmly and repeatedly known in the myths and lore of the Scandinavian, Anglo-Saxon, and to a lesser extent Brythonic peoples. In the face of this well attested evidence it seems somehow unnecessarily complicated to invoke theories about a race living underground (literally and figuratively) since the Stone Age to explain the presence of *wiccedôm*.

Certain features of witchdom and the old way of the Wanes survived in popular folk customs and folklore. These range from the making of so-called corn dollies (symbolic sculptures made from the stalks of grain plants) to sword dancing.

But behind and beyond all of these external manifestations of the old ways is the inner kernel of the timeless reality of the Lord and Lady. While over the centuries some external forms of ritual and customs were being preserved their inner reality was becoming ever more lost to the very people who were maintaining the forms. The distance between the eternal sparks of the God and Goddess and the forms originally intended to nourish them had become very wide by the beginning of the 20th century.

Rebirth

This change, for the practice of *wiccecræft* and the worship of the Lord and Lady, most likely came to fruition in the 1940s and 1950s in England. There were certainly some traditionalists and would-be revivalists of *wiccedôm* who had been in some way involved with the late 19th and early 20th century revival of general occultism and magic.

Across the whole pan-Germanic and even pan-Celtic scenes there had been valiant strides at reviving the high religion of the ancestors throughout the modern centuries. As early as the 1500s in Sweden there were attempts to return to an ancestral Germanic faith of some kind. In this century in Germany many groups had formed to revive ancient Germanic philosophies and beliefs— largely under the influences of Romanticism and Neo-Romanticism.(2) In the Celtic world there had been attempts to revive some form of Druidism in Britain.(3) But none of these represented that part of the old ways which could be described as Vanic or as any kind of witchdom.

One of the earliest impulses in this direction came from the American writer and folklorist Charles Leland who published a curious volume *Aradia: Gospel of the Witches* in 1899. The exact nature of the true sources of this book are hard to determine. It seems to be a semi-learned potpourri of beliefs which support a cult of Italian (more specifically Tuscan) witchcraft. What is most important for us is that *Aradia* shows a predominant role played by the Goddess in the pantheon of witches. Now, while in ancient times the balance between the male and female forms in the Vanic pantheon was probably strong, centuries of official male predominance in the established religion had made the "shock" of strong Goddess orientation a virtually necessary stage.

The impetus for the "revival" of witchdom remained a largely *literary* one for decades. From academic circles came the important, if controversial, works of Margaret Murray. The earliest of these was *The Witch Cult in Western Europe* (1921), which was followed ten years later by *The God of the Witches*. Murray's main thesis is that the witch-cult represents the submerged cultural and ethnic substratum of the pre-Indo-European peoples of Europe. She theorizes that these people literally and figuratively went underground and survived in the myths and legends of the new Europeans as "the faery." These theories were tailor made to be fashionable in an academic setting often dominated by Marxist historical materialism. The whole idea of a suppressed or ethnic lower class going underground to form a cultural resistance movement comes directly out of Marxist thinking. This is also true of the idea of a historical *evolution* from "matriarchy" to "patriarchy"— all very fashionable in early 20th century academia.(4)

Another important literary source for the revival of the belief in witchdom is Robert Graves' "poetic history" called *The White Goddess* (first published in 1946). This work had the rather deleterious effect of positing a practically world-wide Goddess-cult that somehow united the otherwise disparate cultures of the Middle East and Britain. But nevertheless the influence of this book has been enormous in the revival of witch-beliefs.

So for the first four decades or so of the 20th century there had already been building up a whole *theoretical* literature on the cult of witchcraft. It just needed the spark to be realized.

In the world of *practical* occultism only minor attention had been given to "witchcraft" which must have seemed a "crude" sort of magic and religion to the average member of the often well-lettered occult fraternities of Britain. Perhaps two exceptions were to be found in the personages of Charles Seymour and Christine Hartley who were active in Dion Fortune's Fraternity of the Inner Light in the 1930s. Both of these occultists expressed intuitive knowledge "from the inner planes" about the form and content of witchcraft or the "Old Religion" in Britain. It also appears that Seymour and Hartley were Co-Masons, i.e. belonged to lodges which initiated men and women.(5)

The Gardnerian Synthesis

By the mid-1940s there was already enough public information — some of it academic (Murray), some "poetic" (Graves) and some occult (Seymour/Hartley) for a clever person or persons to arrive at an active synthesis. It seems that this synthesis was achieved by Gerald B. Gardner and those who worked with him from 1939 to his death in 1964. Gardner was a retired civil servant who had spent much of his career in India and the east. He had a keen interest in magic and folklore and was also a Co-mason at the same time Seymour and Hartley were involved.

Gardner's synthesis of witchcraft — or *Wicca* [wick-a] as it came to be called and (mis)-pronounced— was a blend of Masonic ritual, what was known from folklore and "witch-hunting" literature about medieval and Reformation Age witchcraft, ceremonial magic (that of the *Key of Solomon* and Aleister Crowley), and general British folklore derived from sources such as Margaret Murray and perhaps later Robert Graves. This synthesis was quite clever indeed. Part of it was certainly blended intellectually and consciously— but much of it probably just seemed "to well up" out of the unconscious realms of Gardner and others around him.

Deeper historical roots to the Gardnerian movement are also to be found in the youth movements of Europe in the late 19th and early 20th centuries. These go back as far as the *Burschenschaft* ("fraternity") movement founded in the early 19th century in Germany by Friedrich Ludwig Jahn and to the *Wandervögel* youth-groups of Germany as well. For a discussion of some of these groups James Webb's *The Occult Establishment* is recommended reading. There was a general "back to nature" edge to these various movements of national regeneration at this time. This is not surprising since these movements were largely borne of Romanticism, which extoled the virtues of the "natural man" and the "noble savage." Sentiments such as these cause the Romantics to praise exotic peoples such as the Amerindians or Polynesians— but really only as a way to point back to their own *natural heritage* from the days before their culture was spoiled by civilization and Christianity.

There were a variety of European youth organizations with this "back to nature in order to regenerate the nation" mission. Among these were the Woodcraft movement founded by Ernest Thompson Seton in 1902, which for a time was allied with the Boy Scout movement. Under Seton's influence Ernest Westlake and his children founded the Order of Woodcraft Chivalry in 1916 and established a "Forest School" on their property at Godshill in the New Forest near London. In 1920 another leader, John Hargrave founded the Kindred of Kibbo Kift (Kentish dialect words meaning "proof of great strength") and also established a camp at Godshill in the New Forest. These organizations, although originally allied with Seton's movement which emphasized the lore of the American Indian, reoriented themselves to a great extent toward Anglo-Saxon and British lore.

Hargrave wrote in his *The Confession of the Kibbo Kift*:

> Thus, in England, The Kindred has sent its roots into a cultural soil which shows most clearly the strata of Anglo-Saxon, Viking, Celt, and the Neolithic builders of barrow, dolmen, and the old straight track. In these traditions it finds something necessary, something clean and bright and true...(6)

These groups, the Order of Woodcraft Chivalry and Kibbo Kift both modeled their rituals on European structures and used Saxon and Norse terms, such as "moot" (meeting), "thing" (assembly) and members took "Woodcraft names." They even practiced nudism— another practice borrowed from the German practices of the day. This extended to their ritual practices as well. Although these groups often disavowed any link to "occultism," their ranks were filled with those who practiced magic and ritual, and there was a clearly *spiritual* as well as socio-political aspect to the work of these groups.

Recent historical evidence clearly reveals a direct link between these movements and Gerald Gardner, who even claims to have made his acquaintance with "witches" in, of all places, the New Forest where both Woodcraft Chivalry and Kibbo Kift were established.(7) For our purposes, what is important to realize is that the "modern witchcraft movement" does have its roots in attempts to regenerate national traditions. That those active in this pursuit would gravitate toward their own *national* symbols and myths, rather than those of the admittedly much admired American Indian, is only *natural*. (It should not be forgotten that etymologically the words *nation* and *natural* are both derived from the same Latin word.)

At some point during the 1930s and 1940s Gardner began to put together his own system under the influence of the aforementioned groups and other occult traditions of a less "folkish" variety.

In the 1950s and 1960s the British tabloids were all aflutter over the revival of witchcraft— which had become technically possible with the repeal of the Witchcraft Act in 1951. Gerald Gardner and others (notably Alex Sanders) took advantage of the eagerly obliging "yellow press" for publicity purposes. (A game all-too-common in the British pop-occult scene throughout this century.) This publicity generated the possibility of a widespread revival of witchcraft. Those of a more traditional background or taste were, however, appear to have been appalled.

Over the past 30 years "Wicca" has grown into a multi-dimensional, manifold tradition— even if it mainly has Gerald Gardner to thank for founding the tradition. For those interested in the history of this fascinating cultural phenomenon recommended books would include Aiden Kelly's *Crafting the Art of Magic* (1991) and Doreen Valiente's *The Rebirth of Witchcraft* (1989). For a more contemporary view of the neopagan traditions in America today Margot Adler's *Drawing Down the Moon* (1987 2nd ed.) is most informative.

Although Gardner may be criticized on many counts, it does seem as though his *magical spell* had its effects on the world. The secret is perhaps to be found in his special operative techniques derived (consciously or unconsciously) old English *wiccedôm*– e.g. ritual flaggelation.

For our purposes the two most important "events" for the rebirth of *wiccecræft* are the creation of Seax Wica by Raymond Buckland and the revival of Odinism or Ásatrú— both in the early 1970s.

Buckland intentionally set out to "create" a "new tradition" with his "Seax Wica." It was apparently not his intention to claim that he had revived the ancient Saxon faith and magic of the Lord and Lady, so detailed criticism or analysis of *The Tree: The Complete Book of Saxon Witchcraft* (1974), as tempting as that might be, would be unwarranted. Suffice it to say that the chief problem lies in his identification of the God with Óðinn (Wôden). Wôden was, and is, the High God of the whole Germanic pantheon— but in the system of *wiccedôm* or the faith of the Vanir it is *Freyr* and *Freyja*, the Lord and the Lady, who are the God and Goddess. There is no Lord but the Lord, and the Lady is his sister.

The second important development of the early 1970s was the revival of Germanic heathenism in Europe (the Armanen in Germany), England (the Odinic Rite), Iceland (the *Ásatrúarmenn*) and America (the Ásatrú Free Assembly and the Odinist Fellowship). A number of these groups were actually somewhat hostile toward "witchcraft"— but that was only because a more holistic vision of Germanic culture had not been developed. In the true elder Troth there was room for the rationalist, the magician, the fighter, and the farmer and craft-folk as well. As it was in essence then, so it should be in essence today.

Again, it is in this spirit of radical diversity that the Vana-Troth, or the true *wiccedôm* (witchdom), is to be founded. Witchdom is, or can be, understood as a part of the more all-encompassing movement known as Ásatrú or simply the Troth (not to be narrowly confused with the organization called the Ring of Troth). But certainly there will be true rings within witchdom which have no official link with any formal religious group. This is just the way things tend to be in organic movements. Organic movements can be difficult to *organize* in an artificial manner because there are certain natural laws already at work giving them shape. Only "schools," "priesthoods," "orders" or "guilds" can be organized *within* such movements.

There have already been several rings of the Vana-Troth or witchdom formed in this country. Although the regular seasonal workings are published in this book, the full initiatory rites used by these rings tend to be unique to certain "schools" or lineages. Although Vana-Troth can be practiced without being part of a personal initiatory tradition (in other words being in a line of succession from an original Vana-Troth leader) such initiations are thought to be most powerful

It is our contention that the *true* Gods and Goddesses of witchdom — the Vanir — naturally *live* within the souls of all those who are descended from their ancient followers. Others may "convert" to the Vana-Troth as well— but it is already naturally a part of the inner constitutions of many. Awareness of the actuality and character of these old divinities can be aroused through the actual performance of rites dedicated to them— or sometimes even by merely reading about their existence in a book of this kind.

What separates witchdom from all other forms of modern Wicca is that witchdom is focused simply on the most ancient and authentic tradition of the Anglo-Nordic Vanir as a religious expression and on the techniques of actual *wiccecræft* as a magical tool— or tool of transformation.

Chapter 2

THE WORLDS OF THE VANIR

The faith and magic of the Wanes does not just weave in and out of the history of *this* world. Beyond the framework of time and space as our five senses are able to perceive them lie other worlds or dimensions of reality. In these realms the Vana-Gods are eternally at home. What is important for true witches of today to realize is that there are seven realms or dimensions of reality with which they must be familiar. These are seven of the nine realms in the whole Germanic cosmology. Witches today must learn about these seven realms and experience their mysteries in as direct a way as possible.

The reason why the Vana-Troth tends to "ignore" the outermost realms of Ásgarðr and Hel is that from the balanced, centered, and orderly perspective of the Wanes these two realms are really equivalent— two sides of the same coin, as it were.

Our most ancient cosmological maps go back to an Indo-European model in which the world in which we live is seen as being in the *middle* of a vast field and sphere of cosmic forces. The "earth" (the manifest universe of three dimensions which can be perceived by the five senses) is not at the "bottom" of the cosmic order— but in the midst of it. We stand at the cross-roads of reality— a realm in which there is more *potentiality* and more challenges than anywhere else in the cosmos.

Other systems, it seems, put our world at the depths of reality and refer to the physical world as "gross matter" or with other almost hateful terms. But to the true witch this world of the flesh is the best of all possible worlds for it maximizes the possibilities for deep and profound experience. This is not to deny the existence of other realms beyond Middlert— or that there is anything necessarily "wrong" with them. Witchdom would rather not put moral labels on what are, after all, parts of a whole organism which in and of itself is holy. The Vanic view is rather pantheistic in that is sees in manifest nature the workings of a divine force.

The favored living symbol for cosmic order among the Indo-European peoples is the tree. A tree is the most profound symbol of the nature of the cosmos because it is organic, ever growing, and even dying but giving rise to offspring through its seed into infinity. It exists on three levels at once: in the dark under-world (roots), on the plane of earth (trunk), and in the celestial realm (branches). In the roots are the dead (past), in the trunk are the living (present), and in the branches those yet to be born (that which shall be).

In the general or Odinic cosmology we know that the cosmos is made up of nine realms or worlds. The tree is called Yggdrasill in the Odinic tradition, but in the Vanic path it is simply called the World-Tree. Also, the nine worlds are not the focus of attention, but rather the seven realms shown in Figure 2.1. In the configuration of the seven realms we see four on a flat plane at the four cardinal points arrayed around Middlert, and one above and one below the "earth plane." These worlds must not be understood as being literally or "physically" at the extremes of these directions. The realms exist in dimensions beyond our world— but we can only make symbolic outer models in three dimensions to help us understand how these realms relate to our world.

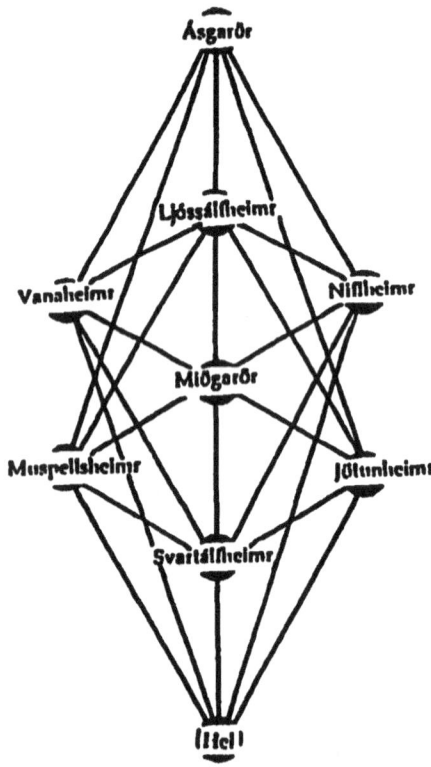

Figure 2.1: The Germanic Cosmology

Wanehame
Vanaheimr

To the west — the direction of the vast waters — lies the world of the Wanes. This was the original home of the God and Goddess. It is the realm of their Father/Mother Njörðr. In Wanehame reside all the powers of the Wanes and from the west these powers stream forth into the world: growth, life, wealth, well-being. In the realm of the senses Wanehame represents taste. Wanehame rules the vegetable and animal — or organic — kingdoms.

Osyard
Ásgarðr

Without ceasing to be Wanes, certain of them made their way into the Osyard, enclosure of the Oses or Æsir. There they became a part of the society of the Oses and exercised their particular kinds of powers among them. Osyard is at the apex of the cosmos— its highest point, and acts as a balance between the forces of the Wanes and those of the Etins. Divinities such as Freyja, Freyr and Njörðr can be said to be both Æsir and Vanir simultaneously. Osyard is, however, not the permanent home of the Wanes, as they are only truly at home in Wanehame.

Etinhame
Jötunheimr

To the east — the direction of moving air — looms the realm of the etins. The exact nature of the etins is explored in more depth in chapter 3. Their cosmological importance is that they provide a certain resistance to the growth and well-being engendered in the west by the Wanes. But the etins must not be considered as "evil" beings. They are the organic balance factor that in fact supports the world of the Wanes as a sort of counter balance. If the west sends forth vegetable existence, the east sends forth mineral existence. Etinhame rules the kingdom of minerals. In the realm of the senses Etinhame represents smell.

Alfhame
Ljóssálfheimr

In Norse tradition this is called "light-elf-world." These elves or alfs are ancestral spirits or divinities of the celestial realms. The Lord, Freyr, is their king. The names Alfhame (or Alphame) or Elfhame are recorded in early documents concerning witches in Scotland. (The name is borrowed from the Norse element in the Scottish culture.) Alfhame is the realm of hyperconsciousness. It is the unknown kingdom of "what shall be." Alfhame stands above and beyond the constraints of time and space, but its shape is influenced by what humans do in Middlert— and in turn the forces resident in Alfhame constitute extremely powerful influences on what can happen in Middlert. The elves are another way of conceiving of the intellect, or patterns of consciousness, inherited from our ancestors

Dwarfhame
Svartálfheimr

Norse tradition calls this realm the "black-elf-world" (or *Døkkálfheimr*, "dark-elf-world"). The term dark elf is another way of saying dwarf. Elves and dwarves are very similar in many ways (see chapter 3). This is the realm of *formation*. In that dimension of reality shape is given to the things we experience in this world. It is the realm of the unconscious or subconscious. Dwarfhame is a largely hidden kingdom of "that which was." It is the *past* which is the primary reality and the eternal shaper of present events and states of being. In Norse mythology the dwarves shape the first "man-like bodies" which were later to be endowed with spiritual gifts by the Gods and thus made fully *human*.

Middlert
Miðgarðr

The "Middle-Earth" is the realm of nature as we know it, the world of humanity — usually bounded by three dimensions and five senses. But it is in this world, which is really the nexus or focus of all the worlds surrounding it, where the highest degree of potential change and development exists. Middlert is the stead of the great challenge. Actions performed in the middle of the world reverberate throughout all the realms. One of the keys to the true witchcraft is knowledge of *how* to make these reverberations and exactly *which* actions to perform in order to make the right things happen or come into being.

In the realm of the senses Middlert represents tactile feeling.

Muspellhame
Muspellsheimr

To the south — the direction of fire — stands the realm of Muspell. It is inhospitable to all but the fire thurses— which are nothing but active embodiments of the extreme forces streaming out of this realm. The realm of Muspell is that of cosmic fire— of infinitely expansive electrical energies. This is one of the two cosmic extremes between which Middlert stands. The other is the cosmic world ice. In the realm of the senses Muspell represents sight.

Niflehame
Niflheimr

To the north — the direction of ice — lies the realm of Niflehame. It too is inhospitable to conscious beings. It is the kingdom of the rime-thurses (ON *hrímþursar*) or "frost giants." These are nothing but incorporations of the extreme force of infinitely contracting magnetic energy. In the realm of the senses Niflehame represents hearing.

Hel
Hel

At the very nadir of the cosmos is the deep enclosure of Hel. This is a realm of death and stasis. It is from this deep well that those things which have died await reconstruction and rebirth. This is a natural part of the way the cosmos, or world-order, works. Hel can receive not only the souls of dead humans, but all kinds of forms of "dead" things"— ideas and objects which await their return. However, there is a similar kind of "holding area" in Wanehame itself which is conceived of as a pleasant realm for organic beings who are awaiting rebirth in the physical realm of Midgard. (For further discussion of "reincarnation" in Germanic lore, see *Green Rûna*.)

* * *

It should be said that the Vanir are most closely associated with the seven "inner" worlds, excluding Ásgarðr and Hel. Further, we might remark that among these seven realms there can be seen arrayed a network of 14 paths or roads (some are often called rivers). These are the 14 mysteries (or secret "things") of the Vanic cult. They are the pathways between and among the various states of being the technique of witchcraft seeks to know— and eventually to influence.

Strikingly P. M. H. Atwater in her imaginative work *The Magical Language of the Runes* uses 14 glyphs which she calls "the runes of Njörd." Several things are important to mention about this system. First, it is an *intuitively* shaped one. The glyphs are not the runes of any historical fuþark system. This speaks for the *possible* inner authenticity of the system because it is most likely that the old Vanic magical system of *wiccecræft* and *seiðr* had *nothing* to do with the runic fuþark. Runestaves and the magical use of them was historically the field of Odinic (Æsiric), not Vanic, *galdramenn*. If you understand the word *rune* in its deepest meaning of "secret" or "mystery" all glyphs or signs which encode secret or magical lore could be called "runes" on some level. The fact that this system is largely *intuitive* and not analytically or historically determined shows its essentially and authentically

Vanic nature. That Atwater identifies this system with the God Njörðr— Father/Mother of the Vanir is also striking. Historically, no *runic* system has ever been ascribed to this deity. Finally, that there are 14 glyphs in the system— which answer to the 14 pathways among the seven realms of the essential Vanic cosmos — seems significant.

The Vanic system would be better served if its practitioners stayed away from intuitive speculation on the historical traditions of the *fuþark*, and Odians would do well in not trying to over-systematize the lore of the Vanir.

Chapter 3

GOD-LORE

Theology

Who are the Wanes, or Vanir, and what do they do in the world? These are the essential questions to ask in any system of heathen theology. This is not to say there will be set and limited answers to these questions which this or any other book or teacher can give. Any answers you are able to arrive at will come from your own *experience* in first asking and then seeking the answers to what you have asked. The term "Vanir" usually only occurs in the plural, the singular form being Vanr. It has no masculine and feminine versions as do the Æsir and Ásynjur, which must also be significant. The term is perhaps related to the Old Norse word *vinr*, 'friend,' and can be compared to Latin Venus (the Goddess of Love) and to Sanskrit *vanas*, who are the 'Gods of Lust'. Clearly then, the Vanir are the friends of humans, and/or of the other Gods, and they are much involved with the ideas of pleasure and love.

Æsir and Vanir

In the ancient Scandinavian sources we learn the "Myth of the First Battle." It is said to be a conflict between two "races" or families of Gods called the Æsir and the Vanir. It should be noted first that this mythic battle is one of *cosmic* or even *psychological* meaning— and is not meant to be "historical" in the sense that we usually mean it. It is the *first war in the cosmos* (ON *fyrsti í heimi*) as sung in the "Völuspá st. 21. This First War is a description of the conflict which is to be expected between two factions or aspects of a dynamic system. It must be remembered that the Germanic folk-soul exults in flux, change and becoming. Conflict is often a part of this process.

The myth of the First War also provides us with a picture of how these natural conflicts are to be resolved in ways both healthy and beneficial to all concerned. The myth itself is recorded in the *Poetic Edda* ("Völuspá" sts. 21-24; the *Prose Edda* "Skáldskaparmál" ch. 57; and in the *Heimskringla* "Ynglinga Saga" ch. 4. The conflict between the Æsir and the Vanir is essentially one of *kind*. That is, there is systemic friction based on their differences in *essence*. We are all familiar with such conflicts in our own lives or within our own selves. We are faced with a situation in which two ways of doing things, ideas or cultures are *essentially* different and seemingly irreconcilable. There is conflict. The Myth of the First War is a myth explaining the archetype or first principle of conflict in the world.

The Æsir and Vanir fight for a long time without a "military" solution. Neither side is able to gain a decisive victory. It is therefore resolved to make a truce in which "hostages" or "pledges" (ON *gíslar*) are sent from each group to the other. This would, in effect, integrate the two groups by knitting them closer together by "blood"— or in *kind*. This, by the way, was the *essence* of "foreign diplomacy and the conclusion of "treaties" in ancient times. Most typically the king would send a daughter to marry the son of the king with whom he had a conflict. Thus they would become bound in kinship ties and future conflicts would become less likely. It was "in the family" now. (The killing of kinsmen was one of the most repugnant acts in the Germanic moral code.)

From the Æsir were sent Mímir and Hœnir, while the Vanir sent Njörðr and Freyr over to the Æsir. (As to how Freyja came to be in Ásgarðr, see ch. 4 under the myth of Heiðr.) The peace was concluded and lasts for eternity.

The Æsir, Mímir and Hœnir, turn out to be a problem for the Vanir, however. It seems that Hœnir, although he was supposed to be highly intelligent, never had anything to say unless the consulted with Mímir. When Mímir was not around Hœnir would always say "Let others decide." The Vanir felt cheated— so they cut off Mímir's head and sent it to the Æsir. (Óðinn preserved the head by magical means and goes to it for counsel in times of need.)

In one version of these events, Snorri Sturluson, writing in the "Ynglinga Saga" section of the *Heimskringla* (ch. 4) says that the Vanir sent Kvasir, the wisest of their kind, as a third hostage. But in the *Prose Edda* he relates another story:

> And they [the Æsir and Vanir] appointed a peace conference and made peace (ON *grið*) by this procedure: both sides went up to a kettle and spat their spittle into it. But when they dispersed, the gods (ON *goð-in*) kept this sign of peace (ON *griðmark*) and decided not to let it be wasted, and out of it they made a man. His name was Kvasir, he was so wise no one could ask him any questions (ON *hluta*, divinatory lots) that he could not solve.

As we will see later, Kvasir has something to do with the science of fermenting intoxicating drink. These sciences are the domain of the Vanir, just as they are of the *Ashvinau* in India. The myth of Kvasir's creation is one in which the *essences* (spittle) of the two races are combined into a living symbol of the peace between them.

The Æsir and Vanir are two poles of one of the many bi-polar structures present in the Germanic (and oldest Indo-European) ideology. These polar opposites are never ultimately seen in terms of absolute "good" *versus* "evil." The Æsir embody the principles of intellect, memory and physical (martial) force; while the Vanir embody the pure essence of vitality, pleasure and craftsmanship. These polarized aspects obviously reflect essential parts of a *whole* society— as well as a whole system of any sort in which consciousness is embodied and alive in an organic, evolving context. No part of this can exist in a healthy (whole) way without the co-operation of the other parts. Conflicts among the parts naturally arise— but can and must be settled in mutually beneficial ways.

The Lord and the Lady

The Lord and the Lady are the true God and Goddess of the witches ancient and true. Polarities exist on many levels and have a multitude of functions. One of the most basic, yet perhaps the most profound, is sexual polarity. Freyr and Freyja express this symbiotic polarity of the sexes the interaction of which gives rise to reproduction and creation of increased vital power. These two forces intertwine and support one another— although each maintains a separate and independent existence beyond or outside the root-level interlace.

Lord and Lady go together like day and night, moon and sun, sea and land. The way in which the two act and interact is perhaps very much akin to the forces *yang* and *yin* in Chinese Taoism— or ,more precisely, related to the way the Indian God Shiva interacts with his eternal consort Shakti. Shakti is the power, the Lord Shiva the power-holder. Some knowledge of Indian Tantrism and the relationship of Shiva/Shakti can often illuminate certain details of the Vanic path.

Freyr and Freyja are twin brother and sister born of the father Njörðr and a "nameless sister wife." Sometimes it is said too that Skaði is their mother. This is all quite mysterious— but we will delve into that mystery in the section on Nerthus/Njörðr below. The Lord and the Lady themselves were known to have had incestuous affairs— which were apparently common enough among the Vanir. All this just further points to the deep-level interlace between the powers and functions of the Lord and the Lady.

It can also be seen that in many ways the Lady and Lord relate to each other as Life to Death. The Lady is expansive, light-giving, and pleasure-giving, while the Lord can be related to death, and withdrawal from life— as the discussion of Freyr and Fróði below will show. However, this withdrawal is always undertaken as a natural and necessary part of the cycle of life. It is the period of the seed's gestation in the dark ground before blooming forth in the spring.

There is no Lord but the Lord, and the Lady is his Sister.

The Lady
Freyja

Freyja — the Lady — is *the* Goddess among the Vanir. No divinity is more important than she in the system of true witchdom.

Freyja is actually a title or divine by-name which means literally "the Lady," that is, it is a royal title of respect. The English word "lady" comes from Old English *hlæfdige*, kneader of bread, or "bread maker." She is the source and medium for sustenance. It is her power which *makes bread*— symbolically and actually. The Old Norse name is derived from the Proto-Germanic *Fraujōn*, which is a royal title: "lady." Her *actual* name is unknown except to her most devoted followers.

Freyja is the embodiment of royal power. Freyr is the wielder of that power, but he does not have the power unless he has her cooperation. The royal power is often seen as incarnated in a queen, who in ancient times was also a priestess (ON *gyðja*). The relationship of the queen to the royal power and of the king to that power is seen in the custom of a new king marrying the widow of the dead king, for example.

Freyja's Names

Freyja has a number of by-names, or *heiti* as they are known in Old Norse. Each tells us something directly of the roles she plays in culture and mythology:

Vanadís, the Divine lady or Goddess of the Vanir, is her name because she is the greatest and most powerful of the Vanir.

Vanabruðr, the Bride of the Vanir, she is called this for her role in the erotic aspects of marriage.

Hörn, the Mistress of Flax (ON *hörr*, flax), is her byname which has to do with her rulership of organic vital forces— especially those vital forces connected with the feminine.

Another Old Norse word for flax is *lín* (linen [made from flax])— which is combined with the masculine force of *laukr* (leek) for magical purposes.

Gefn, the Giver, she is called because of her unlimited ability to provide what people need in life. She is generous with her followers. This name connects her to *Gefjon* (see "Gylfaginning" 35) and to the whole plethora of collective West Germanic Goddesses, known as the Matrones or Matronae, who bear such names as *Alaferhuiae*, "the ones who richly give life-force," *Alagabiae*, "All-Providers," and *Gabiae* "Providers."

Sýr, the Sow, is her name in her warrior aspect. The sow, or female wild boar (ON *svínn*) was a ferocious game animal in ancient times. They were the most dangerous animal a man could hunt. The giant forms of this animal are now extinct in Europe. But in olden times these animals, which were typically hunted from horseback with long spears, could cripple a horse and gore a man to death with its tusks in a matter of seconds. The boar is not only powerful but highly intelligent. It should also be noted that the sow is the leader of the heard, or sounder. The males of the species remain outside the larger society, except when mating.

Mardöll, "She who Shines over the Sea," is her name relating to a watery aspect and to her original cosmic abode in the "western quarter" of the cosmos— *Vanaheimr*.

Gullveig, Gold-Greedy, she is called as not only a ruler of mankind's lust for wealth— which can be a very healthy wish if channelled productively — but also for the *magical* vitality and *light* which the gold symbolizes. We will discuss this in more detail in the myth of Gullveig or Heiðr below. It has also been speculated that the name Menglöð, found in the "Svipdagsmál" st. 3, and which literally means "She who is Glad about a Jewel" (i.e. the *men* of the Brisinga-men) is also a name of Freyja.

Freyja's Animals

Zoomorphic symbols attributed to the Lady give insight into her nature and the way she works in the world.

Cats are holy to her. Although these can come to mean the common house-cat of today, in olden times these were probably *wild-cats* of considerable size and strength. The cats of Freyja should be seen as animals somewhat akin to the bobcat, or even the Norwegian forest cat. In Norse lore they pull Freyja's chariot or wagon. Perhaps the exact species which these cats were supposed to be are now extinct in Europe. These cats, like their domestic sisters, were cunning hunters and ferocious fighters when threatened. They are also known for their essentially "lascivious" natures.

Some scholars have noted, since the cats of Freyja are not given special names in the mythology, that the association with the cat was historically a late one, and perhaps derived from contacts with Asia. For example, the idea of cats pulling a Goddesses' chariot is also common in the Near East, where, for example Cybele is similarly served by large cats.

On the other hand the association with the porcine — the boar, or wild sow — is deeply original. As mentioned above, the boar is a fierce animal. It is intelligent, yet lives close to the earth— rooting *below* the earth's surface for sustenance. In Norse lore Freyja rides a boar to gain access to other worlds. The boar she rides for this purpose is named *Hildisvíni* (battle-boar) and in the "Hyndluljóð" (st. 7) in the *Poetic Edda* this magical boar is said to have been artificially crafted by two dwarves— Dáinn (the Dead) and Nabbi (the Sharp). By means of *Hildisvíni* she can fly from world to world.

The Worship of Freyja

Freyja was certainly the most widely worshipped Goddess in the north as Map III shows. It is likely that several local Goddesses throughout the Germanic territories were absorbed into, or under, the "title" of, Freyja— the Lady. But it would be a denigration of the vitality and multiplicity of the meanings of the Goddesses in the Germanic pantheon to reduce all Goddesses to just one "Goddess." This tendency toward reductionism seems to be a modern monotheistic (or "duotheistic") trend influenced by centuries of Judeo-Christian theologizing, and modernistic eclectic reductionism. In the ancient Germanic pantheon there were several important Goddesses. Although Freyja was indeed the most powerful single Goddess, she was by no means alone.

The greatest single confusion comes with the "collapse" of Freyja with Frigg. This confusion may go all the way back to the time of the demise of official heathendom.

Frigg is not one of the Vanir and was always counted among the original *Ásynjur*— which is the feminine form of *Æsir*. It is interesting to note that the etymology of Ásynjur, sg. Ásynja: <*ans-winjôn, "consort of an ancestral god" (masc. *áss* <*ansuz*), possibly connects this word for Goddess with a possible etymology of the word Vanir, "friends, companions."

Place names associated with Frigg appear to be few and provide little evidence for her cult (see de Vries II:303). It is most probable that Frigg had more to do with domestic and economic management and tranquility than anything else. The names Freyja and Frigg also have nothing to do with each other. Freyja comes from a Proto-Germanic form *fraujôn*, meaning "female ruler." It is the feminine form of Proto-

Germanic *fraujaz meaning "(male) ruler" whence the name Freyr. On the other hand Frigg is derived from a Proto-Indo-European root *preih-, meaning "to like or love" the Proto-Germanic form would have been *frij-jō, which would mean "the dear or loved one." Strictly speaking, Frigg is the Goddess of love among the Ásynjur, Freyja was this, *and more*, among the Vanir.

So, as a Goddess, what does the Lady do? She really expands and extends herself throughout all of the great aspects of divinity. She rules over organic (animal and vegetative) cycles of vitality and reproduction (although she herself is seldom seen as a "Mother Goddess") and she rules over cycles of cosmic change. The symbol of her relationship over these cycles and the magical tool by which she manifests her power is the Brisingamen— the necklace of the Brisings (four dwarves). The myth of how she acquired this instrument is told in chapter 4 below. She also rules over a warrior function. This is shown by the belief that half of the slain on the battlefield were collected to her hall, called *Folkvangr* (plain of the warrior band)— while the other half went to Óðinn's hall called *Valhöll* (hall of the fallen). The Lady is also the great mistress of magic— especially of that form known as *seiðr*. So Freyja rules over aspects of production, war and magic. She could therefore be fervently worshipped by farmer, warrior or magician alike. Probably no other single deity in the Germanic pantheon — in masculine or feminine form — is as broadly worshipped in society through such a breadth of functions as the Lady.

Obviously the worship of such a far-reaching deity could be used for a wide variety of human concerns and needs. If you need to cause positive change — to bring wealth, prosperity or well-being into your life — Freyja can be called upon. If you need love or erotic liaisons of any kind, Freyja will be friendly to those biddings. If you need victory in battle, Freyja may be called on. If you need to increase your magical power or knowledge, Freyja will hear and answer your call.

The Lady has been found to be a great divine role model, or exemplary model, for female magicians working in the northern tradition. It should be added that the magic that Freyja has to teach is *significantly different* from that taught by Óðinn. Freyja is not merely Óðinn in a dress! For example, historically Freyja had nothing to do with runestaves. Hers is the magic of the pure holy sign and song, the witchcraft of the offerings, dance and orgy and other means of raising ecstatic states. She holds the secrets of herbs and other magical substances.

In connection with the story of Freyja's teaching the art of *seiðr* to Óðinn, found in *Ynglingasaga* (ch. 4) we read that: "[Freyja] was priestess at sacrifices [*blótgyðja*]. She first taught the Æsir sorcery [*seið*], such as was practiced by the Vanir." Further on in chapter 7 of the same saga we read:

> Óðinn had the skill, that brings greatest power, and worked it himself. It is called *seið*, and by means of it he could know the fate [*ørlög*] of men and foretell events that had not yet come to pass. He could work the death of men or loss of luck [*hamingja*] or sickness. So also could he take the wits and strength from some people and give it to others. But this magic [*fjölkyngi*], as it is worked, involves such great perversity [*ergi*] that it is thought by manly men to be most shameful to practice it, and this art was taught to priestesses [*gyðjur*].

Here we have a catalog of the magical powers Freyja taught to Óðinn.

In the ancient northern European cult of the saints in which the old Gods and Goddesses were worshipped in Christian guise, Freyja corresponds to St. Lucia (Lucy)— especially in her aspect of Heiðr/Gullveig. *Lucia* means the "light-filled," as Heiðr means "shining one." It is also true that the legend of St. Lucia (probably not historical material) there are three attempts to kill or violate her— including burning. Again this would have matched old Scandinavian beliefs about Heiðr. St. Lucia's festival of light on December 21 (Mother Night) is especially important in Scandinavia. Other saints who correspond to Freyja in other areas are: Walburga (Valborg) and Mary Magdalene.

The Lord
Freyr

Freyr — the Lord — is, with his father Njörðr, one of the high Gods of the Vanir. As far as witchdom is concerned, Freyr is by far the most important male deity.

Freyr is really a title or divine by-name which means literally "the Lord," or "ruler." The English word "lord" comes from Old English *hláf-weard*, the loaf-guardian. What the power of the Lady (loaf-maker) produces, the Lord guards and dispenses to the people. Again we see that the Lady is the power, and the Lord is the power-wielder.

As opposed to Freyja, whose *true* cultic name is secret, the name of the Lord (Freyr) is thought to be Ingwi or Yngvi. The name of Ingwaz obviously goes back into deep antiquity, as Tacitus reports the folk-name Ingaevones in the first century CE. Ingwaz/Ing is the name of the twenty-second rune in the elder and Old English rune row. "The Old English Rune Poem" reads:

> [Ing] was first   seen by men among the East-Danes
>   until he went east again
> over the wave he went,   the wain followed on;
> this is what warriors   called the hero.

In later Scandinavian tradition the two names, Freyr and Ingvi, were again brought together in the compound title Yngvi-Freyr, or Ingvi, the "Lord of the Ingaevones." This must be an old formula, as we also find it in *Béowulf* (l. 1319): *frea Ingwina*, "Lord of the Friends of Ing."

The etymology of *Ing-* is disputed. It may simply be a word for "man," related to Tocharian *en≥kwe*, perhaps really "the mortal one," or it may be a metonymic name indicating the phallus— connected to the Greek word *ónkhos*, "spear." This is an aspect found connected to both Freyr and Óðinn. A famous image of Freyr shows his erect phallus, and the description of the temple at Uppsala says of the image of *Fricco*, or Freyr, as *"cum ingenti priapo,"*— with an enormous priapus.

Ingvi is the Earth God. In northern tradition Freyr is also known as *veraldar goð*, God of *this* World. His name also became closely associated with the legendary king of Denmark named Fróði. The name Fróði literally means "filled with life-force." Under the rulership of Fróði the whole of the northern world lived in a golden age of peace and prosperity. This is called the Peace of Fróði (ON *Fróða friðr*).

Freyr is a mythic model for the divine king in certain parts of the North. The institution of the divine kingship is well-known and well documented in the Germanic tradition— as it is in the Celtic. The north seemed to differentiate somewhat among three types of divine kings: the Tyric, the Odinic, and the Vanic (Freyr). The Odinic divine king was prevalent in the southern Germanic territory while the Vanic divine king was most often found in Sweden.

The *Ynglinga Saga* (ch. 10) includes the detail that Freyr, conceived of as a mythic Swedish king, was not burned when he died, and his death was keep a secret, and tribute was paid to him in order to continue good harvests and peace in the world. Similarly, in Book V of the *History of the Danes* Saxo Grammaticus reports that the mythic king, Fróði III of Denmark was embalmed upon death and his body was driven around the land in a wagon, as had been done with him in life, in order that he might continue to provide the land with his blessings of vital power.

The cosmic abode of Freyr is uniquely in *Ljóssálfheimr* — or Alfhame — for he is said to be the king of the Light-Elves, or simply elves. It says in the "Grímnismál" (st. 5) in the *Poetic Edda*:

> In days of yore   the gods gave to Freyr
> Elf-home as a "tooth-fee."

The "tooth-fee" (ON *tannfé*) was a token given to a child when it cut its first tooth. Thus the ultimate origin of the common custom of a "fairy" exchanging a child's baby tooth for a coin can be seen.

Freyr's Animals

Three symbolic animals are associated with Freyr: the horse, the boar, and the stag. Of these, the horse is also attributed to Óðinn— but the other two are more uniquely Vanic.

In the literature we actually learn about certain horses, typically named Freyfaxi or Freysfaxi (Freyr's maned one) in *Hrafenkels Saga* and in the *Vatnsdœla Saga* which were worshipped as incarnations of the Lord. This is the important magical and religious difference between the way in which the Germanic folk revered divine animals and the way, say, American Indians might believe in true *totem* animals. To the Teutons the animals were either *symbols* (manifestations of essential characteristics) or *incarnations* of the transcendental God or Goddesss. The animal was not in and of itself divine, nor was the *animal* thought to be the divine progenitor of the clan (as is the case in true totemism)..

It is in the aspect of the stallion as a sexually virile and vital creature that the power of the Lord is seen to be most manifest in it.

The boar is Freyr's most unique animal. The Lord is said to have a boar named Gullinbursti (Golden-Bristled) or Sliðrugtanni (Cutting-Tusked) which was, like Freyja's boar, fashioned by a dwarf. In the Yule-tide festival of old a boar called the *sónargöltr* ("sacrificial boar")— was slaughtered and eaten by the gathered folk after oaths had been sworn on its head— or "bristles." Here are the origins of both the "Christmas ham" and the "New Year's resolutions" of popular culture. Remember that the boar was a great symbol of royalty and of ferocious battle-spirit to some tribes of the ancient Germanic folk. So Freyr was also the "Tusked God."

But he was also (or alternatively) the *Horned God* associated with the hart or stag. In the myth recounted in chapter 4 about Freyr's wooing of Gerðr, he is said to give up his sword— and so is left with only a hart's horn with which to fight at Ragnarök. With this horn, or antler, Freyr is also said to kill the giant Beli (*Prose Edda*, "Gylfaginning" ch. 23). The mythic Vanic king Fróði was said to have been killed when he was gored by a hart or the horns of a "sea cow." Heroes attached to Horned Gods often are said to be killed by horns or tusks. In this way the God is "reclaiming" them. So Freyr is also the "Horned God." There are also several associations of Freyr with horned cattle.

The Lord is also known to possess a wondrous ship called Skíðblaðnir— also made for him by the "sons of a dwarf." Snorri tells us that this ship is so immense that all the Gods can board it fully armed— yet it can be folded up so small that it can fit into a small bag. When it is in action it always has a following wind (*Prose Edda*, "Gylfaginning" ch. 43). Remarkably this vehicle sounds like a fourth-dimensional device for traversing the extra-dimensions of space— by "folding" space/time. It is a self-propelled fourth-dimensional vehicle. The dwarves are indeed a clever sort.

Worship of the Lord

Historically Freyr was one of the most widely worshipped of the Gods in the north. Map IV clearly shows this. In those areas where Freyr (or Freyr and Freyja together) was supreme the Lord took on a wide variety of divine functions— many having to do with war and with sovereign rulership (of men as well as of the natural cosmos). So he may have absorbed some of the aspects of other Gods on a local basis. The Lord does *not*, however, seem to have had much if anything to do with the practice of operative magic— this seems to be Freyja's domain among the Vanir as it is that of Óðinn among the Æsir.

The Lord, or Ruler, wields and directs the force and power of vitality — the life-force — *embodied* in the Lady. As the ruler or wielder of vital force he is also the God of agricultural management and planning. As the ancient Germanic folk believed the warrior impulse to be a manifestation of divine vital power or strength, the role of Freyr as the ruler of cosmic vitality was easily transferred to a warrior function among his war-like followers. However, it is important to note that weapons — and especially *metal* (iron) weapons — were not allowed within a temple or sanctuary made holy to Freyr. One of the ways these temples were defiled and de-sanctified by churchmen and their sympathizers upon the coming of Christianity was to throw a spear or other metal weapon into the sanctified area. The principle of rulership of vital power could also be extended to the rulership exercised by divine kings. Their very *beings* — the power which they held or embodied — was the principle by which ruled. Other divine kings might be evidenced by the decisions they made or the things they did— but the Vanic divine king was evidenced by the prosperity and peace his rulership brought to the land. This Vanic type of divine king is very much like the Celtic idea of the role of the king and his relationship to the land.

Devotees of the Lord can call upon him for a wide variety of human needs. Snorri tells us ("Gylfaginning" ch. 24) that Freyr is the ruler over rain and the shining of the sun and the produce of the earth, and that it is good to call on him for prosperity and peace (ON *til árs ok friðar*). He therefore rules over the wealth (*fésæla*) of humans.

In the tenth chapter of the *Vatnsdœla Saga* there is a passage which gives a clue to a practice of placing gold or silver tokens dedicated to Freyr under the posts of a house. There a Finnish sorceress prophesies to Ingimundr that he will go to Iceland from Norway and:

> There you will become a man of rank and grow old. Your family will be large and renowned in that land. . . and it shall happen as I said, for there is a sign [*mark*] of this (i.e. the truth of the prophesy) in that the talisman [*hlutr*] King Haraldr gave to you at Hafrsfjord has now disappeared from your pouch and has gone to the very same place where you will settle, and on the talisman [*hlutr*] (an image of the God) Freyr is marked in silver, and when you raise a homestead there the truth of my words will be proven.

Archaeologists have in fact found such tokens at the bottom of postholes of Viking Age houses and temples.

In Christian times the worship of Freyr was absorbed into St. Hubertus, patron of hunters, whose symbol was a stag, as well as into Christ— who took over the Lord's title: Old Norse *Freyr* and Old English *Frea*.

Nerthus/Njörðr
Mother/Father of the Wanes?

It is most likely that there was originally lore of a bisexual entity which was able to engender offspring from itself. Such lore is quite common in Germanic tradition. There are at least two other examples: Ymir the cosmic giant does this in Eddic mythology, as does Tuisto mentioned by Tacitus in the

Germania (ch. 2). Tuisto's very name probably refers to its nature which contains the male and female components "twisted" together.

This may account for the fact that early on we find a Goddess named Nerthus, and later on we find a God named Njörðr— both apparently derived from the same original name. (It is, however, not necessary to assume that the two names are the same divinity. They may reflect two different deities, whose names simply appear similar— after all, the form Nerthus is from a source around a thousand years older than those attesting Njörðr.)

The fact that it is said that Njörðr fathered Freyr with a "sister," who is not named, lends some credence to the idea that this was an act more of self-regeneration than simply an act of incest— which is, as we know, a common enough practice among the Vanir.

The meaning of Njörðr's name is also perhaps relevant to practice Vanic. Although the name has been connected to the Celtic word *nertos*, meaning "force," or "power"— especially vegetative power, as well as to Greek *nerteroi*, which refers to the concept of the underworld and even to Lithuanian *nerti*, "to submerge," and *nerieti*, "to spawn"— it was once most evocatively connected to Sanskrit *nart*, "to dance." Edgar Polomé once linked this to the idea of the dance as a ritual way of raising power— which fits with certain ideas about the practice of *wiccecræft* as a way to raise power through circular dances, and so on. Again, the idea that in this technique is found the origin of the Vanic divinities is a telling one.

In the "Gylfaginning" of the *Edda* (ch. 23) Snorri describes Njörðr in the following manner:

> The third God (*áss*) is the one who is called Njörðr, he lives in that heaven which is called Nóatún. He rules over the course of the wind, stills sea and fire, and is to be called on for seafaring and for fishing. He is so wealthy and rich that he is able to bestow abundance of land and riches on those who call on him for this. <Njörðr is not of the Æsir kin.> He was brought up in Vanaheimr, but the Vanir gave him up as a hostage to the Æsir, and accepted as a exchange-hostage one named Hœnir. He brought about reconciliation between the Gods (*goð*) and Vanir.

The name of Njörðr's abode, Nóatún means "boat-town." Certainly Njörðr was very much attached to the wealth of the sea and coastal towns. Map V which shows the place names associated with the name of Njörðr also demonstrates that his cult was largely a water-based one.

Other interesting facts about Njörðr are that in "Grímnismál" (st. 16) he is called the "blameless (god)" (ON *meinsvanr*), and is specifically mentioned ("Vafþrúðnismál st. 39) that Njörðr will return to Vanaheimr after Ragnarök. Although Njörðr is obviously most connected to matters of wealth and prosperity, perhaps because war could often be very profitable, there are several instances of the name of Njörðr used as a part of a kenning for a "warrior" or "king." Among these is *Sig-Njörðr*— "Victory-Njörðr."

Other Divinities

Although some of the deities of the high mythology — the kind recorded in the Eddas — received no sacrifice or cultic worship, many of the so-called lesser divinities such as elves, dwarves, dises, and even etins did enjoy a lively cultic observation. This was especially so at the household level of the religion. It should perhaps be kept in mind that the true practice of traditional Germanic religion, be it Vanic or Æsiric, is best expressed at the level of the *household*. Ours is primarily a home-centered religion.

The deities of hearth and home are the wights linked to the house and most especially to the people in the home. Strictly speaking these wights are not classified as Vanir or Æsir. They form other classes altogether. But they remain important for the regular practice of the Vanic way. The household wights are perhaps more closely linked with the Vanic path than with the Æsiric one simply because the home, land and basics of life — the substance of the household wights — are more essential to the Vanir than the Æsir.

In olden times the faith and craft was practiced most intensely at the level of the household. Since this is really the way it tends to be today as well— when it comes to witchdom — it is at this level of practice where a great deal of the authentic essence of the old ways can be recovered.

The Wights

Elves

The elves (ON *álfar*, sg. *álfr*) are a complex group of entities. They dwell in (Light)Elf-hame and are often associated with Freyr who is said to rule over them in their abode as their king. The word "elf" literally means "the shining-white one." These are entities of light (not always seen because they *can be* exceedingly small in stature) who sometimes interact beneficially and sometimes maliciously with humans. Essentially, they are the collective light-bodies or "minds" (ON *hugar*) of the ancestors (in their female forms they are called dises). These beings continue to have contact with the minds of humans. They have much lore and wisdom to teach. They are the mental faculties of the ancestors that have been reabsorbed into the cosmic organism but which remain differentiated from it as a whole.

Dises

The dises (ON *dísir*, sg. *dís*) are the feminine counterparts to the elves. In the oldest level of the terminology there would be no female elves— just dises. Of all of these so-called "lesser" entities, the dises perhaps enjoyed the most active level of cultic attention in ancient times. Two of the main northern holy festivals, Winter-Nights and Disting, were especially dedicated to them— and secondarily to the elves. The word "disting" really means "assembly of the *dísir*."

These entities ensure the continued prosperity and fertility of the household. They keep the children safe and the household healthy and harmonious. They are not known by individual names, but are always referred to as a collective body. They form a part of a parallel social universe.

The possible etymology of the term may connect it to Sanskrit *dhishaná*, "divine female figure," related to Sanskrit *dháyati*, "sucks [milk]" < PIE *dhā- "to give."

In some respects the dises can be seen as beings which are very similar to the *bansidhe* [banshee] of Celtic tradition.

Dwarves

The dwarves are also known in Old Norse as *svart-* or *døkk-álfar* ("black"- or "dark-elves"). They are said to dwell down below Middlert in Svart-Álf-hame. These entities too have much lore to teach, but their main work in the world is that of craftsmen or fabricators of physical reality. They are the shapers of shapes that come into being in Middlert. They are always thought to be the forgers of magical weapons and other wondrous objects— they made Freyja's Brisinga-men, and Freyr's ship Skiðblaðnir, for example. In the everyday household cult they can be considered the reabsorbed skills and crafts of the ancestors expressed in a mythic and cultic form. Dwarves are the spirits of craftsmanship— although in later popular terminology the word "elf" appears to have been used for both elves and dwarves.

Etins

It might come as somewhat of a surprise to some that the etins, or "giants," were the focus of a lively cultic life in the ancient North. This is because the "giants" are so often considered to be the enemies of the Gods (especially of the Æsir). But it was the case that the giants — especially female ones — enjoyed the sacrifices of the rural and farm folk of the ancient north.

To understand why this was so, it is first necessary to explain something of the "giants." Actually in Old Norse lore there are three distinct kinds of giants. All three are often misleadingly translated with the same term: "giant"

One type of giant are the thurses (ON *þursar*, sg. *þurs*). These beings are embodiments of certain cosmic principles of a physical or natural character. They are unchanging processes relatively devoid of consciousness. They are thus portrayed as being exceedingly *stupid* although they may contain great storehouses of knowledge in the form of intrinsic patterns waiting to be unlocked by conscious entities. They are of great age, as they are as old as the origins of the cosmic order itself. Thurses are indeed older than the Gods and so can have much to teach them— but the thurses are by their very nature *hostile* to the Gods and Goddesses because they are the forces of entropy and unchanging mechanism in the world. The rime- (or "frost") thurses and the fire-thurses are the most primal and powerful of this class of beings. Thurses are not worshiped or honored.

The rises (ON *risi*, pl. *risar*) are simple minded beings of enormous physical stature. If any of these are likely to represent the pre-Indo-European inhabitants of the north, it would be the rises. They are often beneficent, beautiful to look at (although just as often ugly), and sometimes are said to intermarry with humans. The rises are not worshipped either.

It is the etin (ON *jötunn*, pl. *jötnar*) who are often worshipped and honored by humans in localized cultic activity. The rises are purely physical and organic beings, the thurses are vast non-intelligent cosmic forces, while the etins are a complex lot. As a class of beings they are neutral in the contest between the forces of consciousness and non-consciousness in the universe. Some are allied with the forces of consciousness (Gods and humans) while others are allied with the thurses. They are of great age and strength— although they can actually be conceived of as being of any size. Female etins often have beautiful forms and are alluring to human men. Because they have absorbed the wisdom of the æons through which they have existed, they are vast treasure-houses of information and knowledge. However, they usually can make no use of this knowledge themselves.

Etins are given gifts in order to assure their beneficent interaction with humans and with the forces of nature in which they are enmeshed. They are usually worshipped at outdoor shrines in remote natural locations, such as mountains and seascapes in the general vicinity of the home.

Worship of the House-Wights

It is thought that the best way to worship, or give honor to, the house-wights, or those of near-by mountains or bodies of water is to leave small (sometimes symbolic) gifts on harrows or in shrines specially constructed for them.

They will most appreciate gifts of food and drink. These should be left in open containers (earthenware bowls, for example). The ritual of giving to the wights is simple. Place the gift on the harrow or in the shrine and from the heart ask that the wights "take well with the gift." This is a way of asking them to accept it graciously from your open heart.

If the gifts are left outdoors, they should be left for a period of 24 hours (usually left around the time of sundown). If the gift has been devoured it is a very good sign that the wights have taken well with it— if not, it may not be an unfavorable sign, just an indication that it should be taken back into the home again. If the gift is food or drink it should be given to the children of the house to eat, or to family pets.

Regular worship of the "lesser divinities" is an important part of the Vanic way. This, perhaps more than the regular observation of the great festivals and rituals, forms the everyday substance of the true northern faith.

Chapter 4

THE MYTHS OF THE VANIR

There are a variety of powerful myths concerning the Vanic deities preserved in Old Norse literature. But this represents only a small fraction of the total mythic material that must have been once available about these Gods and Goddesses. The sad truth is that most of the Vanic mythology was either suppressed by church authorities, or was simply not recorded in the Old Norse poetic tradition largely dominated by Odinic interests.

Still, with all that, there is a great deal of material recorded in the Eddas about the Vanic Gods and Goddesses. For although the whole body of mythology may indeed have an Odinic bias to it — since the mythology was recorded in writing by poets and Óðinn is the patron of poets — because the mythology is seen as a great *whole* by the true Odinist (or Odian) the Vanic mythology does get its fair share of attention within the whole. However, we can not fool ourselves into thinking it would not have been somewhat different if we had a "Vanic Edda" before us instead of an Odinic one.

Those interested in the older mythology of our folk and ancestors have for the most part been too reliant on retellings of the myths. It is best really to go directly to the sources themselves. But at the same time, the sources are often somewhat obscure and difficult to understand (and often hard to find). What we will do here is give some literal retellings of the most important Vanic myths along with specific references to the Eddic and other sources for the myth. When dealing with books that attempt to "retell" the myths it is usually the case that if a given part of the story is not to be found in the Eddas or sagas the authors of these retellings are probably making things up off the tops of their heads to "make the story flow better." But all we can assume is that perhaps the story was meant to "flow" in just the way the ancient authors wrote them. In addition to the bare bones retellings, we will include exact sources in the Eddas or other literature where you, the reader, can see the original material more easily.

It should be noted that the retellings below are couched in the past tense. This is not to imply that the mythic events are not still being manifested today and throughout time— it is just that in the Germanic way the *past* implies more *stability* and a certain high level of *eternal being*. However, the whole process of how the mythic realities interact with the ever-becoming present moment and the yet unformed sea of time beyond is a celebration of the eternal flux of ultimate reality.

The Myths of Freyja

Gullveig-Heiðr

What is said to be the cause of the First War in the Cosmos — the one between the Æsir and Vanir? This seems to be tied up with a mysterious Goddess who came from the side of the Vanir to the stronghold of the Æsir. She was called Gullveig— her name may mean something like "Greedy-For-Gold."

She was not greeted well by the Æsir in Óðinn's hall. They tried to kill her with spears and after piercing her— they burned her body. But after they had killed her and burned her she rose up again and made herself known. So again the Gods pierced her body with spears and again they burned her. However, even after this she rose up once more for a third time. After this third time of rising up she was transformed into an even more powerful deity and lives even now— but she is no longer known by the name Gullveig, but rather Heiðr. Her new name means the "Bright One." It is a name often used to describe witches (or seið-wives). But the Vanir were offended that one of their own had been treated in this ill manner. So they demanded tribute for the violent acts of the Æsir. The Æsir refused, and thus the First War began.

The battle went on for some time, with neither side able to gain a decisive victory. So it was finally decided to call a truce. In order to establish this truce, the Gods, both Æsir and Vanir, agreed to exchange hostages. The Æsir sent Mímir and Hœnir, while the Vanir sent Njörðr and Freyr.

But who was the mysterious Goddess from the Vanir, at first known as Gullveig and later as Heith? The answer might be clarified once one realizes that Freyja — who is always counted with the Vanir who now live among the Æsir — is *not* one of the deities exchanged in the truce negotiations. The question is then *how* did Freyja come to be among the Æsir? One answer is that Gullveig or Heiðr is none other than Freyja herself. Thus she holds a special place among the Vanic deities who now dwell among the Æsir: She is the one who came *of her own free will* and underwent the ordeals of the Æsir and was not destroyed, but rather was transformed, by them.

The main source for this myth is the "Völuspá" in the *Poetic Edda*.

Freyja and the Brisingamen

Here we will simply give the direct translation of the material in the obscure "Sörla Þáttr" which tells the story of Freyr's acquisition of the necklace or girdle in a most straightforward way:

> The land east of (river) Vanakvisi [= 'Vana-branch'] in Asia was called Asialand, or Ase-Home, and the people who dwelled in the capital city they called Ásgarðr were called Æsir. Óðinn was named king over them. That was a great place of sacrificing [ON blótstaðr]. Óðinn established Njörðr and Freyr as sacrificial priests [ON blót-goðar]. The daughter of Njörðr was Freyja. She went with Óðinn and was his mistress.
>
> There were some men in Asia, one of whom was called Álfrigg, another Dvalinn, a third Berlingr, and a fourth Grerr. They had their home not far from the king's hall. These men were of the kind who burned to lay their hands on everything. This sort of man people called dwarves. They lived in a stone. They mingled with people more then than nowadays.
>
> Óðinn loved Freyja very much and in those days she was the fairest of all women. She had a chamber (a small building attached to the main hall) that was so fair and strong that people said that if the door was shut and locked then no man was able to get in without Freyja's will.
>
> One day Freyja went to the stone, it was open. The dwarves were forging a golden necklace. It was exceptionally beautiful. Its looks pleased Freyja very much, and Freyja's looks pleased the dwarves very much. She asked to buy the necklace and offered the dwarves gold and silver and other precious things. They said they were not lacking money. They said each one of them wanted to sell his part in the necklace and wanted nothing other than for her to lay with each of them for his night. And whether she thought this deal was for better or worse, they agreed to this. After the passing of the four nights and the completion of all the terms, they handed the necklace over to Freyja. She went home to her chamber and was silent about that which nothing was said."

The necklace (or in some accounts it is a belt or girdle) is an object by which Freyja has great power over the wealth of the world and over the workings of nature. This seems to stem from the very nature of the necklace and its origins. Most probably the four dwarves are the forces of the fourfold cyclical nature of all things which are born, live, die, and are reborn. On one level the dwarves mentioned may be identified with the four dwarves at the four cardinal points of the world: Norðri, Austri, Suðri and Vestri (whose names obviously mean the four directions: north, east, south and west). The names are different here, but such is often the case. There is one correlation between the names of the dwarves we have in the "Sörla Þáttr" and the four cardinal directions, however. Dvalinn is the name of one of the dwarfish shapers of the Brisingamen, and the name of one of the for harts around the World-Tree which gnaw at its leaves (the other hart-names being Dáinn, Dúneyr and Dýraþrór).

It is further said concerning the Brisinga-men that it was soon stolen by Loki at the urging of Óðinn who had become jealous of Freyja's possession— and the manner in which she got it. As Loki could not normally get into Freyja's chamber, he turned himself into a fly to gain entry, and then into a flea to unclasp the necklace itself. But Freyja was able to gain the jewel back when she agrees to help Óðinn in the continuation of the unending struggle of the warriors of Midgard.

Sources for the myth of Freyja's acquisition of the Brisingamen are the "Sörla Þáttr," Snorri's fragmentary references to it in his *Edda*.

The Rune of the Brisingamen

Here the word "Rune" is being used in the sense of a "mystery," not a character of symbolic lore. The Brisingamen is to the Vana-Troth what the *Valknútr* is to the Runic system— a mysterious operative key to the system.

As with many other things, the beginnings of the understanding comes though a close reading of the lore. It has been noted that the four *dwarves* who forge the Brisingamen share a name with the cosmic harts and that it is not unlikely that the four dwarves are therefore likely to be identified with Norðri, Austri, Suðri and Vestri. Concerning these dwarves we read in the description of the creation of the world that the gods (*Gylfaginning* ch. 8): "They also took [Ymir's] skull and made out of it the sky and set it up over the earth with four points, and under each point they set a dwarf. Their names are Austri, Vestri, Norðri, Suðri."

These dwarves are creative, shaming forces at the four corners of the cosmos which hold up or sustain the vault of heaven or sky. They are the fulcrum-points for regulating the forces of the natural order, and knowledge of them provides knowledge of the natural cosmos.

A reflection of this is ritualized, even for modern Wiccans, in the celebration of the seasonal rites and the rites for the establishment of a "circle" in which to work. The obvious, or exoteric, aspect is embodied in the *ring*, the circular form, as one moves though natural time from north to east, to south to west and back to the north: that is, from winter to spring, and on to summer and eventually to fall and back to winter. However, the quoted text above gives the directions and dwarf-names) in another order. It is typical of esoteric Germanic thinking to look at things as polar opposites to be synthesized, and here we see it once more. The directions are given as east-west-north-south, which creates another internal flow of force different from the external cyclical or circular one. This esoteric flow is reflected in the mysteries of the Vanir.

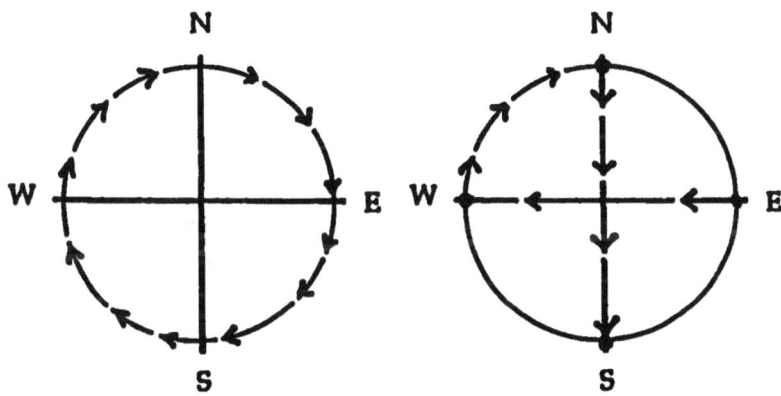

Freyja and Óðr

Freyja's true husband is a God named Óðr. Some say he is one in the same with Óðinn of the Æsir. This may well be for Óðinn is known to have taken many names— and Óðr is the pure power of inspiration of which Óðinn is the master.

Óðr was a great traveller and he would often go out on long journeys into unknown lands and worlds. When he went he would always leave Freyja behind in her own land where she ruled. But Freyja longed after Óðr and wept bitterly— the tears that rolled off her cheeks were of the purest red gold. It is for this reason that the skalds so often call gold "Freyja's tears."

Freyja sometimes took to searching over the land and throughout the worlds for Óðr. Where ever she would go she shed her tears, and so gold is scattered throughout the world. When she was on her own journeys seeking the hiding places of Óðr she would often have to take on other names herself— for this reason the Lady is known by many different names in the many lands of the world.

It appears that this search for Óðr is an unending one for the Lady— but that in her travels she always gains in power and extends her rulership. She spreads the possibilities for desire and sows the seeds of discord throughout the world by the tears of gold she sheds. In doing this she ensures the continued dynamic flow of energies in Midgard and throughout the other worlds. In his "Skáldskaparmál" in the *Edda*, Snorri provides a multitude of kennings for gold relating to this idea of gold being "Freyja's tears."

Sources for this myth are to be found in the *Heimskringla* and in the *Prose Edda*— both by Snorri Sturluson.

The Myths of Freyr

Freyr and Gerðr

It is said that once the God Freyr went to Ásgarðr and seated himself on Hliðskjálfr from which he could see into all the worlds below. In the realm of the etins he saw a beautiful etin-maid who was opening the door to a beautiful building. When she opened the door light shone out from her arms over both the sky and sea— "and all the worlds were made bright by her." When Freyr saw this sight he fell at once in love with her. The maid is named Gerðr. Her father is Gymir and her mother is the etin-wife Aurboda.

Right away the Lord sent for his trusted servant Skírnir, whose name means the shining one. This is perhaps an active aspect of the Lord himself. Freyr asks Skírnir to go in his stead to ask for the hand of the fair etin-maid. To do this Skírnir needs Freyr's horse to cross the barriers between the worlds— but he also asks for Freyr's sword in payment for the errand. To these conditions Freyr agrees as he is so lovesick for the fair etin-maid.

Skírnir arrives in the realm of the etins, but at first can not gain entry into the maid's abode because it is guarded by fierce dogs. When the maid sees Skírnir she invites him into her place and asks him if he is one of the elves, Æsir or Vanir. He denies that he belongs to any of these and offers her eleven golden apples of everlasting youth to say that she returns the love of Freyr.

But Gerðr refuses the gift and rejects the love of Freyr. So Skírnir offers her a better gift— the ring Draupnir which increases itself by eight every nine nights. This is the same ring that was burned on the funeral pyre with the God Baldr. This too Gerðr refuses, saying she has quite enough of gold in her father's hall.

At this point Skírnir's patience has worn thin and he threatens Gerðr with the sword of Freyr, saying that he will cut her head off with it. At this Gerðr too becomes angry and says that her father will kill the impudent youth if he finds him there. Upon hearing this Skírnir launches into a long curse formula which threatens the maid with the most dire consequences if she does not give in to the love of the Lord.

The curse formula has its magical effect and brings Gerðr to her senses and she agrees to meet in nine nights time with Freyr at that place called Barey— "for true love a trysting glade."

Although Skírnir's mission has been a success, when he reports to Freyr that it will be nine nights before he can meet the maid the Lord responds with the heart of a love-sick soul:

>Long is a night,   longer are two—
>   how shall I suffer for three?
>Shorter to me   a month often seemed,
>   than half of this wedding-eve.

Afterward, Gerðr is counted among the Goddesses.

The main source for this myth is the "Skírnismál" (also known as the "För Skírnis") in the *Poetic Edda*. A version of the myth is also given in the "Gylfaginning" of the *Prose Edda*.

The Slaying of Beli

Snorri tells us that Freyr's gift of his sword to Skírnir is the reason why he has to use an antler to slay the giant Beli— and he must also fight with only this antler at the final battle during the Ragnarök when he must fight the giant Surtr ("the Black-One").

The source for this obscure myth is may be discovered in both the *Prose Edda* and the *Poetic Edda* (where Freyr is simply referred to as "slayer of Beli" in the "Völuspá" st. 52.

The Myths of Njörðr

The Myth of Njörðr and Skaði

This myth ties into one about Loki who once abducted the Goddess Idunna and took her and her apples of youth everlasting to etin-home. He did this to pay off a debt he owed to an etin named Þjassi, whose abode was Þrymheimr in etin-home..

When the Gods begin to grow old and decrepit due to the absence of Idunna's apples, Loki was called before them and commanded to return Idunna and her apples to their rightful place in the realm of the Gods and Goddesses.

Loki agreed under duress to do this— but he asked for Freyja's falcon-coat to transform himself into a falcon so he could fly his way to the mountainous etin-home. This he was granted and he flew down to the land of the etins and found that Þjassi was not guarding Idunna at that moment so he transformed her into a nut and grasped her in his falcon claws and flew off back in the direction of the realm of the Gods. When Þjassi found that Idunna had been taken, he flew after Loki in his eagle-shape. After Loki landed safely among the Gods, they set a fiery trap for the eagle and burned his feathers when he flew through the gates of the holy enclosure. Then the Gods killed the wounded Þjassi.

Now, Þjassi had a daughter named Skaði. She took up her armor and weapons and set out for the realm of the Gods to avenge her father's death. But when she arrived the Gods offered her compensation, or weregeld, for her father. This compensation was to take three forms. Óðinn would take the eyes of the dead Þjassi and cast them into the heavens to make two stars. We perhaps now know these stars as Castor and Pollux in the constellation of Gemini. Also the Gods said they could make the sad and dour Skaði — who was bent on revenge — laugh. This they did when Loki tied a rope around the beard of a goat and the other end around his balls. In this way Loki and the goat played at tug-o-war until both were squealing loudly. Afterward, Loki dropped into Skaði's lap and she was caused to laugh out loud.

The most complex sort of compensation, however, was that the Gods promised Skaði that she could pick one of their number to marry. However, she would have to pick her future husband by looking at his feet only. When she looked at the feet of the Gods, she choose the most beautiful looking feet— thinking they must belong to Baldr the Beautiful. But much to her disappointment they turned out to belong to Njörðr of Nóatún.

This was an ill-fated match because Njörðr needed to live by the sea to be happy and Skaði needed to be in her mountain home-land. At first they agreed to spend nine nights at one place, and the next nine nights at the other. But neither could be at all happy in the abode of the other. When Njörðr came back from the mountains of Þrymheimr he said:

> Loathsome are mountains to me, I was not there long—
> only nine nights:
> the howling of wolves seemed hateful to me
> beside the song of the swans.

And when Skaði returned from the sea-side she said:

> I could not sleep on the bed of the sea
> because of the screaming of birds;
> that one wakes me who every morning comes
> from way out at sea.

So after a while, the two decided to go their separate ways, with Njörðr in his abode, and Skaði in hers. In some traditions, however, Skaði is indeed said to be the mother of the Lord and the Lady.

Sources for this myth are to be found in the *Prose Edda*, the *Heimskringla*, and in the *Poetic Edda*.

Another myth is alluded to in the "Lokasenna" (st. 34) where we read that Loki says of Njörðr: *"Hymis meyjar höfðu þik at hlandtogi ok þér í munn migu"* ("Hymir's handmaidens had thee as a urine-pot and pissed in thy mouth"). Hymir is an etin who has his abode far in the east, and who is the keeper of the great cosmic brewing kettles. (See the "Hymiskviða" in the *Poetic Edda*.)

These few fragments of the ancient Vanic mythology tell us that there was once a vast storehouse of images and tales— many of which have now been lost to the textual tradition. Some of them may be recovered through the use of folklore. For example, many of the tales collected in the early 19th century in Germany by Jacob and Wilhelm Grimm — the so-called "fairy tales" — contain a great deal of Vanic material. Essentially, these are tales handed down from one generation of (usually female) story-tellers to another. The magical and religious concepts still stored in the *Kinder- und Hausmärchen* is a vast field still waiting to be ploughed.

Chapter 5

CALENDAR OF THE WICCAN WORKINGS OF THE TRUE

Wiccan workings are based on the *turning* or *twisting* of the cycle of the year. The Germanic year is divided into two main halves — Winter, or the dark half of the year, and Summer, or the light half of the year. The Winter is of the Lady, but ruled over by the Lord, while the Summer is of the Lord but ruled over by the Lady. By the same token the northern magical conception of the day is that the Sun is a Goddess, Sunna, who rules over the day-time sky which is masculine, while the night-time sky is feminine, but ruled over by the God, Máni, the Moon.

This conception of the seed principle of anything being contained in the depths of its opposite is very ancient and found throughout many levels of Germanic thought. In some ways it might be seen as being akin to the principle of *yin-yang* in Chinese Taoist philosophy. It ensures a virtual balance of forces within an eternally dynamic and ever changing world. The flux of change and becoming is something the northern mind celebrates in the wiccan year. The pattern of the cycle, or the passageway through which change takes place, is the static or constant element in the system. But it is virtually *hidden* except to the initiate who knows its path and its ways. It remains generally invisible to the physical eye.

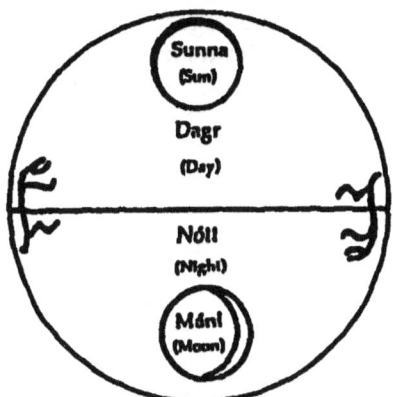

Figure 5.1: The Germanic Model of the Day Cycle

The day is divided into eight parts, also called airts. The sky and earth are also divided into these eight segments in Germanic lore.

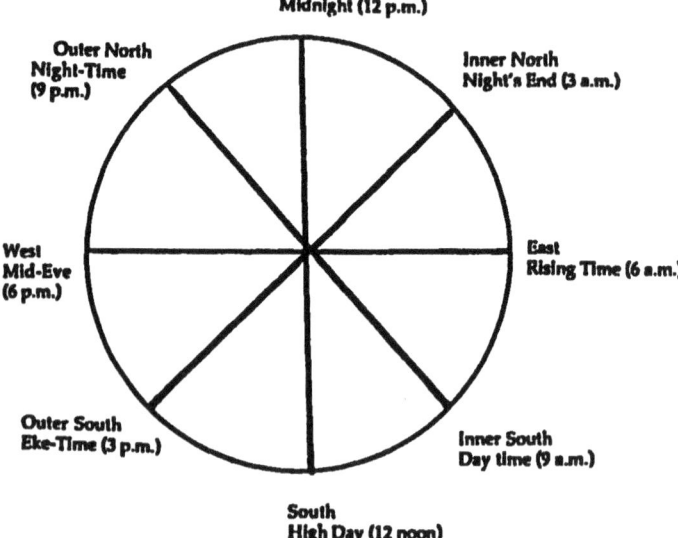

Figure 5.2: The Eightfold Division of the Sky and Day

In ancient days the exact times of some of these would vary according to the season and the geographic latitude of the observer. Midnight and High-day are always constant. But for modern pragmatic practice this standardized model will be most useful.

By the same token the year is also divided into eight parts. Again in ancient times the exact times for these divisions, and the rites which accompanied them, varied from location to location, and from tribe to tribe. This is only pragmatic since much of the significance of the old calendar was derived from the meaning it had for the organic cycle of the agrarian year.

For example, Easter (Germanic Spring) is the first sign of blossoming of organic life after the Winter-tide. This naturally occurs earlier in southern Germany than in Sweden, earlier in England than in Iceland. So the true sign of Spring (Easter) would actually be some *organic* sign— the first flower to appear in a sacred field, or the first robin of Spring, etc. This would signal the time to begin the rites of Spring. It could come a bit earlier in one year, a bit later in another. This was more accurate and real than keying rites to purely mechanical events in the heavens.

What remains stable is the number and order of the holy events in the cycle. Even if we do not observe the tides in the same organic fashion of the ancestors, we still maintain the sacred cycle. That is what is important anyway. The eightfold cycle of creativity and generation is the thing at work here. It is not just significant for an agrarian society— all things in nature undergo cycles of existence. The wiccan year is the true experience of these cycles leading to an inner mastery over them.

The current crop of popular Wiccan, or sometimes would-be Celtic, writers have little knowledge of the ancient wiccan calendar. There is abundant information on this in Scandinavia — especially in Iceland where in the countryside folks still tell time in the old ways — but only vestigial remains of it in the purely Celtic context. The main way it becomes obvious that the modern wiccan tradition is in fact ignorant of the old ways is that the so-called "solar" festivals (which correspond to the major Anglo-Saxon festivals of the year) seem to be copies of the so-called "lunar" ones. Thus *Samhain* [SAW-en] has virtually the same significance as Yule (ON *Jól* [yohl] or OE *Giule* [yooleh]). If we go back to ancient times we would see that these differences are largely due to climatic differences between the "original homeland" of the Celts in central Europe and that of the Germanics in northern Europe and Scandinavia. Neither people was particularly "hung up" on impractical celestial events— such as equinoxes and solstices — such things as the first robin of spring were much more important. The "reason" for this is simply that the British wiccans confabulated the Celtic and Germanic systems when in fact the eightfold division is one system of continuous cycle— not a superimposition of one cultural system on another.

The fact that these events could vary in time points to the reality that it is the rhythm — the number and intervals of the tides and rites — that is essential rather than their exact mechanical timing. Therefore the wiccan workings can vary from ring to ring.

Although the real significance of the eightfold division is in the inner process of cyclic development, it is perhaps still best illustrated from the example of the agricultural year. This is because in the economy of an agrarian (or hunting/herding) society the very practical survival of human beings is keyed to an understanding of these cycles of existence. In today's economy, especially in America, there is little recognition of the continued necessity for the experience of the cycles for our own psychological well-being and even survival.

The wiccan year is divided into eight parts as shown in Figure 5.3. The names of the festivals represent a synthesis of the old English and the Norse influence as it was felt in the time just before the Norman Conquest in 1066 CE. It should be remembered too that Germanic culture remained dominant in the countryside in England long after the Conquest as well— it was, however, no longer the culture of the governmental establishment.

You may notice that there are few differences between the wiccan calendar of the Wanes and the calendar used by the common troth, or Ásatrú. This is because ultimately they do belong to the same greater tradition. But their modes of expression are significantly and sometimes radically different.

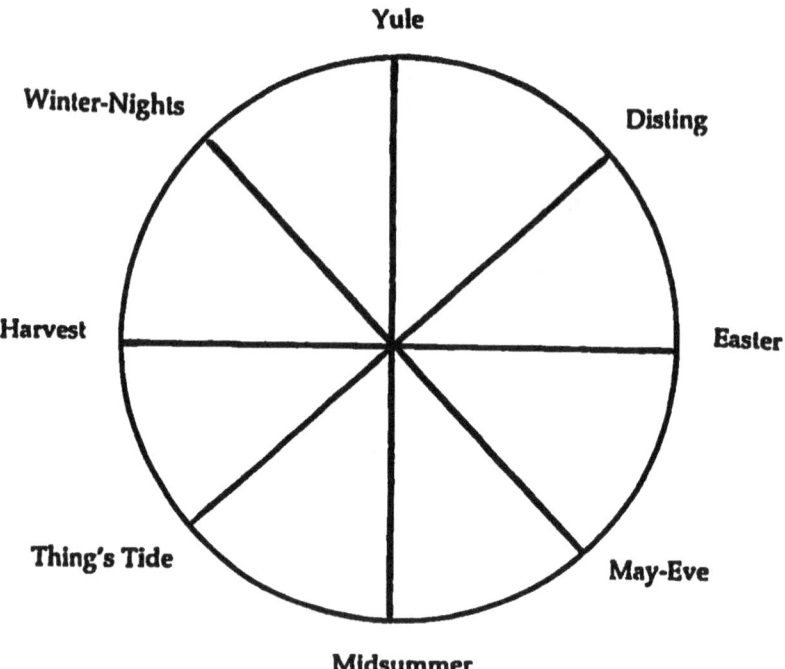

Figure 5.3: The Wiccan Year

The power of the cycle is intrinsic and its origins transcend the natural universe. The natural cycles which we observe around us in the world are reflections, or manifestations, of the unseen and mysterious cycles just outside or beyond our senses. This is the key to why those are wrong who object that we cannot practice true witchdom today because culturally we have been separated from the natural agrarian cycle. Such a protester is only half right. From the natural perspective we have been alienated from the cycles of agriculture and animal husbandry which stood at the center of much of ancient life and symbology. But once we realize that these natural phenomena are themselves *symbols* of more mysterious cycles we realize too that perhaps "liberation" from the natural cycles was necessary for our evolution to step beyond these boundaries.

In fact the eightfold cycle is a nine-termed system. The center represents the ninth— which is the *subject* of the cycle. That is, the center is the actual one undergoing the effects of motion through the outer eight terms. The mysterious relationship between nine and eight is illustrated by the fact that if you divide the ring or circle into 360 (3 + 6 + 0 = 9) equal parts (or degrees) and mark it off into eight equal divisions you will have 45 (4 + 5 = 9) degrees in each eighth (airt). Also, if you count the sum total of degrees as you move around from 0 degrees to 360 degrees you will discover that at each of the points of the airts (every 45 degrees) the number of degrees will be reducible to nine (e.g. 45° = 4 + 5 = 9; 90°; 135° = 1 + 3 + 5 = 9). This is just a symbolic way of refocusing on the *subject* of the process— the ninth in the center.

Dates given in the following discussions are approximate, because traditions vary from place to place.

The Yule-tide (ab. 20 December - 31 December), or vertical axis where space/time bridges to the realm of the Gods, is the gateway between the ring and the center, or between eight and nine, or between one and nine. In Yule the cycle begins and ends. With the Yule-tide exist the last (9th) and the first. The end of the Yule tide marks the beginning of the hidden cycle. The Yule tide begins at a time around the winter solstice (20 December), which is called the Mother Night, and lasts for twelve nights. That twelfth night is Yule proper, and the previous twelve nights are the Yule-tide, or "yule-time." The symbolism is why we celebrate this time as the new year. Esoterically Yule represents a total rebirth in the darkness and stillness which comes at the end of a cycle of becoming. There is great inner or *psychic* renewal— which is brought about through extensive contact with the ancestral beings. The mythic formula which provides the ritual for this time is found in the *Prose Edda* (chs. 51-52 and 85).

Disting (about February 14) is a time which is particularly sacred to the Wanes. It is named for to honor the *dísir*, female ancestral beings who govern the cycles of nature. They are also given special honor on the Winter Nights, and they, or beings like them are the "mothers" referred to on Mother Night. The time of Disting is a time when the ground is prepared for planting (sowing). This preparation is largely an act of "purification." This purification is really an act of *strengthening*. The physical vehicle to be transformed (the earth or the body/self) is subjected to excesses and inversions of normal behaviors in order to, so to say, "exorcise" detrimental forces.

Old heathen practices still survive in the central European celebrations of Karnaval (as it is called along the lower Rhine) or Fasching (as it is called along the upper Rhine and in the Danube region). In French-speaking areas this is called *Mardi gras*. During this time there was an excess of sexual activity and all kinds of inversions of normal behavior were practiced— women dressed as men and men as women, the jester took the throne and the king played the fool. The mythic formula for this working is found in the *Prose Edda* (ch. 59).

Easter (about 21 March) comes at a time close to the spring equinox. Historically lunar considerations have also been important to the timing of this festival. (Note that the Roman Catholic formula for determining when Easter is to take place is that it is to fall on the first Sunday after the first full moon after the spring equinox.) Easter is the time of the rebirth of light— it is the actual *manifestation* of the renewal of the soul physically prepared for at the time of Disting. The mythic formula for the Easter working in the Vana-Troth is provided by the *Germania* (ch. 40).

May-Eve (April 30) is the time of the full blossoming in the physical world of the seeds planted at Disting and which had their sprouting at Easter. This is a time when the spiritual and physical worlds are blended in a particularly potent way. In Germany this time has long been known as *Walpurgisnacht* (Walburga's Night), and it has been recognized as the "witches' night" *par excellence* in central Europe for just as long. The mythic formula for the celebration of May-Eve is found in the *Prose Edda* (chs. 59 and 68).

Midsummer (about June 21) is the day and night of celebration of the full zenith of both physical and psychic power. The planted seeds have reached their full growth and are at the height of their power— but they are for the most part yet unripened. The mythic formula for Midsummer festivities is found in the *Prose Edda* chs. 61 and 97).

Thing's Tide (about August 23) is an interval of rest and relaxation. It can also be a time when there are intense interactions between persons and a time of deep inner reflection for each individual. This is when gatherings of several rings together to form a *thing* or "council" take place. It is a time to recount the traditions of the rings and in a real sense *recreate the world*. The mythic formula of the Thing's Tide is found in the *Poetic Edda* in the "Völuspá".

Harvest (about 23 September) is the time in which the rewards of the cycle are reaped. The planted seeds have reached their full maturity and the time is ripe to gather in the fruits of the efforts of the year (cycle). The mythic formula of Harvest is illustrated in the *Prose Edda* (chs. 62 and 89)

Winter-Nights (around 14 October) is the time of the end of the cycle accomplished through the inner "threshing," that is the practice of separating out what is beneficial from that which is unbeneficial in life. The wheat is separated from the chaff. The nourishing grain is stored in a safe place within, to be drawn on for nourishment throughout the coming year— while the chaff is left to be blown to the eight winds. The mythic formula of Winter-Night is found in the *Poetic Edda* in the "Hyndulj óð".

It must be borne in mind that most of these tides represent the *end* of a time span that has gone just before. The notable exception to this is the Yule-Tide which clearly marks both the beginning (Mother Night) and the end (Yule) of the specific twelve-night span of time which makes up the entire Yule-Tide. But in a real sense the end of the Yule-Tide marks the beginning of Disting, which concludes on the festival of Disting itself which falls around 14 February, and so on. Therefore the activities and qualities which characterize the festival times should be carried out and observed all during the time preceding the festival tide.

The Ritual Formula of Witchdom

A book cannot give you the practical experience of witchdom. It cannot initiate you into the ways of witchdom— that must be done in the flesh, in the world of this earth. What this book can do, however, is provide the basic ritual formula that underlies the ancient forms, and which may help explain the origins of some of the modern Wiccan ritual formulas.

Wiccan Ritual Format

I. *Wayfaring* (Processional)

Worship

II. *Ringing* (Setting a Circle)
III. *Song* (Hymn to the Deities = invocation)
IV. *Play* (Enactment)
V. *Saw* (Declaration)
VI. *Weave-Work* (Litany)

Work
(Festivities)

VII. *Witching* (Dance/Song/Chant)
VIII. *Gifting* (Offering or "Banquet")
IX. *Leaving* (Closing)

Merry Making

The **wayfaring** brings the folk together from far and wide to assemble at the appointed place and time to worship and celebrate their kinship and fellowship with the Gods and Goddesses. This is a *processional* of the celebrants of the given festival from a starting point to the place of the actual working. In some real sense this is accounted for magically by the trip taken by each celebrant to get to the place where the festival will take place. But symbolically this aspect is usually re-enacted near the working site. Ideally the wayfaring would start near a more "civilized" area and move into a more natural area where the ring is established. In this way there is a definite movement from order into the realm of chaos, or disorder of elements out of which the wiccans will weave a new order in accordance with their ideals. It is a movement from the outermost level of reality to the innermost center of existence out of which all things come. Psychologically it is a movement from the realm of the conscious — through the subconscious — into the collective unconscious (also called the super-conscious) realm wherein the archetypes dwell. The **worship**, which originally meant "to give worth, or value" to something or some one, consists of five parts. This second part of the formula is intended to bring the divinities and wiccans together. First a ring in which the Gods and Goddesses may manifest with the folk is established. Then there is the singing of a **song** in praise of the divinities and call them close and into fellowship with the wiccans. Next there is the enacting a **play** — a symbolic drama with or without words — based on the mythical pattern of the season. After this the **saw** is used to declare in no uncertain terms what the purpose of the working is. The play tends to be non-verbal and the saw a verbal version of the same idea. Finally the folk and the deities are integrated, their wills made one, through a **weavework** done by means of a lead and response litany of the divinities and their attributes.

The **Work** is really more a "play of creation." It consists of a circle or ring dance accompanied by a magical chant, by which power is raised. The power is raised in a neutral way— to create a substance with which to work. This is the **witching** in its most essential aspect, and probably the technique from which the whole school of magic gets its name. There is then a symbolic convivial meal in which the folk consume food and drink and share it with the Gods and Goddesses they called to be present with them. The part that is given to the divinities is the **gift** or sacrifice. At the conclusion of this part of the rite, the participants retire to another area to continue **merry making** and to consume more of the gifts of the Gods in various forms. In this last part of the formula is where orgies of sexual play were often enacted— that play which so horrified the monks of the Middle Ages.

Clearly it can be seen that the medieval accounts by anti-witchcraft propagandists are reflected in these formulas. The medieval reports, as hostile as they were, also have the advantage of being more contemporary with the actual practices in question.

Actual working groups, or rings, of the Vana-Troth or Witchdom are made up of individuals who have been initiated in person by members of pre-existing rings. Their individual rites and the words which accompany them will, of course, vary, but the overall level of authenticity of their lore will generally follow the formula given here.

This formula is used as a regular form of observation of witchdom. Otherwise the followers of the Vanir also participate in the *blótar* of the general Troth or Ásatrú. Followers of the Æsir and Vanir worship in common at least three times a year, although the Vana-Troth can also hold separate celebrations— as do Odians of the Rune-Gild, or other members of other specialized groups within the greater troth movement.

Chapter 6

WICCECRÆFT AND SEIÐR
The Magical Ways of the Vana-Gods

In ancient times there was little formal distinction between what later came to be called "magic" and "religion." However, "magic" or "sorcery" was typically distinguished by a number of technical terms, whereas "religion," for the ancient Germanic peoples, was characterized as *loyalty* (troth) to one's ancestors (ultimately to the Gods and goddesses) and adherence to proper customs. The religious practices of the Vanic cult differ little from that of the common Æsiric cult. The customary ceremonies, as outlined in *A Book of Troth* cover this aspect. In the field of *magic* or operative work, the situation is more complex.

The ancient Northerners divided "magic" into two large categories— in Old Norse these were called *galdr* and *seiðr*. At some points in history much was made of the distinction between the two, while at other times the distinction seemed less important. *Galdr* is a verbal-symbolic kind of operative activity, which through the willed manipulation of signs is able to have a direct effect on the world. This is what Rune-magic is. This is the kind of "magic" with which the Æsir operate.

Another kind of operation deals with substances, energies and spirits or wights, and almost always involves the induction of a trance-like state of consciousness. In the north this was historically called *seiðr*, while in the southwestern Germanic region it was called *wiccecræft*. We know a great deal more about *seiðr* than we do about *wiccecræft* due to the voluminous material provided by Icelandic literature.

The practice of *magic* is of extreme importance to the Vana-Troth, or religion of the Vanir. Magic is the "technology" by which the individual and/or group are able to assume some power in their relationships with the world and other people. This part of the Vana-Troth is especially important to those who are followers of Freyja, in whose cult magical practices are most prevalent. But to explore this part of the way of the

Wanes it is extremely important to understand precisely what we are talking about when we use the term "magic." "Magic" itself is, of course, a foreign and fairly modern term in English. Our ancestors who practiced *wiccecræft* would not have known the term. By knowing exactly what terms were used, and what practices the terms connoted, we will be able to know a great deal about their beliefs and workings. Otherwise, what tends to happen is that would-be believers in modern "witchcraft" fill in the "unknowns" with their own personal fantasies, or prejudices— or modern occult practices. What we want to do is fill in the "unknowns" with "knowns" as much as the record allows. This will mean that our journey into the truly mysterious will be as well informed as possible.

The two terms which will dominate our considerations are Old English *wicce-cræft* (and its derivatives and variation) and Old Norse *seiðr* (and its derivatives and variations). There is much talk about these words, but often little real information.

The Historical Relationship of *Wiccecræft* and *Seiðr*

In general it seems that *wiccecræft* and *seiðr* are in what scholars call "mutual distribution." That is, originally at least, where one was found, the other would not be present. This is usually because the terms cover the same ground of meaning, or their meanings are so similar that they are both not needed. *Wicce(cræft)* is, of course, Old English. The fact that there is a surviving German word *wicken*, meaning "to practice soothsaying," tends to show that the word was brought with the continental Saxons to England in the fifth century.

Unfortunately, we have very little literature of a heathen flavor in Old English— so we don't have examples of the use of *wiccecræft* which much suggests a pre-Christian context. Most examples of the use of the word seem to be where the Anglo-Saxons were translating Latin (usually Christian) texts, where we see it was used to translate terms such as *veneficium* (poisoning, sorcery), *necromantia* (necromancy), or *divinatio*(divination). However, the fact that the word also exists in continental Old Saxon attests to the fact that it is an ancient word.

Seiðr is Old Norse. It is a kind of magic explicitly connected primarily with the Vanir, and most explicitly with the Goddess Freyja. Luckily we have a wealth of pre-and non-Christian contexts for the word in the Old Norse *Edda* and various sagas.(8) There is also perhaps an Old English word which was derived from *seiðr*, or which may be an Old English cognate: *sidsa*, "a kind of bewitching" and there is a word *ælf-siden* meaning "night-mare." The literal meaning of the last word seems to be something like "elf-bewitchment."

In chapter one we saw why it should not be considered unusual that was a cross-fertilization of words and beliefs of this kind in England. After all parts of this country, along with Scotland, were under Scandinavian (Norwegian and Danish) political and cultural domination for about 200 years at the close of the Ango-Saxon period of English history. (See Map II for some indication of the areas of heavy Scandinavian influence.) It seems logical to assume that there was a cultural exchange of ideas and techniques of magic between the Scandinavians and English. This exchange would have been greatly facilitated by the fact that the Scandinavians and Anglo-Saxons shared a common cultural and linguistic ancestry. This despite the fact that the English were at least nominally Christianized by the time of the Scandinavian invasions, which began in earnest in the mid 800s. The attestation of the word *sidsa* might be just one indication of this exchange.

Wiccecræft

The etymology of the root word *wicc-* in Old English is a matter of great debate. One etymology connects it to the idea of *twisting* or *turning*, and links it to other words such as "wicker," and so derives from Proto-Germanic *wik-. This may be a reference to the circular or turning dance used in the practice of witchcraft. Another etymology connects it to the Proto-Germanic root *wih-* 'sacred'— which connotes something set apart from the profane. Semantically these two etymologies might fit together at the point where we reconstruct an enclosure — perhaps made of wicker-work — used as a way to set apart sacred space and inside of which a circular dance was performed in order to excite the vital energies necessary to the performance of the operative acts.

The uses of the term *wicc-* in Old English are not extremely helpful. Most of the instances are what are called *glosses*, that is, places in generally Latin texts where an indigenous word has been written or scratched as a translation.

Wicca (sorcerer) glosses Latin *sortilegus* (lot-reader, soothsayer), *magus* (magician), *pythonicus* (magician, seer), and *conjector* (interpreter). It is paired with other Old English words such as *drý* (sorcerer < O.Ir. *drūi*, knowing certainly), and *wíglere* (soothsayer).

Wicce (sorceress) glosses such Latin terms as *pythonissa* (seeress), and *parca* (goddess of fate). It is paired with *wælcyrige*, which is the same term as found in Old Norse *valkyrja*. Here it appears that it is not a reference to a supernatural feminine being, but rather to a human sorceress, perhaps of the kind referenced in Ibn Fadlan as an "angel of death."(9)

Wiccecræft glosses Latin *necromantia* (necromancy) and *veneficium* (poisoning, sorcery), and is paired with *drýcræft*. In Old English Leviticus 20: 27 (which reads in the Vulgate *vir in quo pythonicis vel divinationis fuerit spiritus*) is simply translated *se man begâ wiccecræft*— "the man who practices witchcraft..."

The importance of the liturgical element of a ritual *dance* to the practice of *wiccecræft* is an enduring one. Old English *lâc* can mean a sacrifice or gift, *lâcan* (Go. *laikan*, ON *leika*) means "to dance," Old High German *leih* means "song; rhythm." this sacred dance was a vigorous — and in many instances probably a sexual — one. Tacitus in the *Germania* (ch. 24) writes of naked youths dancing between swords and spears. Similar dances were mentioned in the 15th century and have continued into modern times (see mummer's dance). Of course, Pope Gregory reports (*Dialogs* III:28) that the Langobards sacrificed a goat's head "to the devil" while dancing in a circle and singing "terrible" songs. Most intriguing is the report of Saxo Grammaticus (*Gesta Danorum* Book VI) concerning the behavior at the sacrifices at Uppsala among the "sons of Freyr"— which are said to involve "womanish body movements, the clatter of actors on the stage and the soft tinkling of bells."

Even if the contexts of the term *wiccecræft* in Old English are not particularly helpful, we can be happy that there appears to have been a rich vocabulary surrounding it. Additionally, comparisons with the apparently related system of *seiðr* in Scandinavian can be instructive.

The Vocabulary of *Seiðr*

There is much to be learned by studying the words used by the ancient Norse to describe and modify the form of magic or sorcery they call *seiðr*. The word occurs in two forms, both *seiðr* and *seið*, which are both grammatically masculine words. The variation between *seið* and *seiðr* may be dialectical. No satisfactory etymology for the word *seiðr* has been offered. Such an etymology could link it to other Indo-European words so that a sense of its underlying meaning could be inferred. It is unlikely that it is to be linked to *seiðr*, "a kind of fish, *gadus virens*"— besides no semantic corroboration is forthcoming. It is most likely that the noun is has been derived from the strong verb *síða*, "to work sorcery," the simple past tense of which is *seið*, "I performed sorcery." There is also a weak verb (*seiða*) of identical meaning which appears to have been derived from the noun at a later time. There is also a phrase: *seiða seið* "to work sorcery." The vibrant and rich history of the word makes it appear that the word is fairly old in the language, and that it has not been recently borrowed from a neighboring language. It is perhaps a vestigial form from the pre-Indo-European lexicon.

Germanic magic has always been conspicuous by the fact that as many men as women seem to have been involved in it. (More men than women were executed for witchcraft in Iceland in the "witchcraft-craze" of the Reformation Age, for example.) Therefore we find the word *seiðmaðr* (*seið*-man) right beside the feminine *seiðkona* (*seið*-woman). There is also a pejorative masculine term *seiðskratti* meaning "(vile) wizard or sorcerer."

The sagas and Eddas provide us with a rich vocabulary regarding the equipment used in the performance of *seiðr*. We learn that there is a *seiðhjallr* ("sorcery-platform") which may be set up at a *seiðstaðr* ("place where sorcery is performed"). This *seiðhjallr* is often described as being of great size and as being high. Sometimes *seiðmenn* do not use a specially constructed platform, but rather just go on top of a house. The important thing seems to be that they are elevated up off the ground. Sometimes too, the *seiðmaðr* may carry a *seiðstafr* ("sorcerer's staff"). One word for sorcerers was *seiðberendr* i.e. those "bearing" or "carrying" *seiðr*. As the staff is an object which might be carried, and taking into account *grafseiðr* as a kenning for a serpent in the "Old Icelandic Rune Poem," and the link between the idea of a serpent and a magical staff (cf. also the Jörmungandr, the "great magical staff" as a kenning for the cosmic serpent, *Miðgarðsormr*, it is possible that the word originally refers a magical staff or wand of some kind. But lending credence to the idea that the original meaning of the word *seiðr* had something to do with a vocal performance is the technical term *seiðlæti*, which is a plural construction meaning "the sounds heard during the performance of *seiðr*." It is tempting to identify these sounds with the vocalizations which survive among central Asian "throat-singers."

In chapter 37 of the *Laxdæla saga* we read a powerful and remarkable report of these *seiðlæti*:

> [The sorcerers] climbed onto the roof of Hrútr's house and made great sorcery [*seiðr*] there. When the sound of the sorcery [*seiðlæti*] arose the people inside were at a loss to make out what was going on, but the singing [*kveðandi*] was beautiful to hear. Hrútr alone knew this sound and asked that no one look outside that night. "Let each keep himself awake who can, and no harm will come to us if we do as I tell you. They all went to sleep anyway. Hrútr stayed

awake the longest, but he also fell asleep. Hrútr's son was named Kári and he was twelve years old and the most promising of Hrútr's sons. Hrútr loved him very much. Kári hardly slept at all, for it was against him that this sorcery [*seiðr*] (MS var. *leikr*, "sport") was directed. He did not feel much at ease. He got up and looked out. He walked into the sorcery [*seiðr*] and fell down dead.

On a side-note, anti-*seið* magic is also mentioned. In chapter 28 of the *Göngu-Hrólfs Saga* we find the term *seiðvilla*, which apparently indicates "a (rune?-)stave to counteract sorcery." The phrase *rísta seiðvillur*, "to carve staves to counteract *seið*" is used.

Etymology of the Word *Seiðr*

It must be said from the outset that the etymology of the Old Norse word remains unknown. It is likely that the noun *seiðr* has been derived from the past tense stem of the strong verb *síða*. Which doesn't help us much in unraveling the underlying meaning of the concept, as that verb is equally without etymology. It is perhaps a word derived from the underlying "pre-Germanic" language, or one borrowed from a neighboring language— the original word now having been lost in that language.

One thing I must vigorously insist on is that the word *seiðr* can in no way be connected to the English word "seethe." The Old Norse word cognate to "seethe" (i.e. "boil") is *sjóða*, which means "to boil, seethe; forge; brood over something (*sjóða eitthvat fyrir sér*)." The Old Norse word is a strong verb with the principal parts:

sjóða, sýð; sauð, suðum, soðinn
"to boil, (he) boils; boiled, (we) boiled, pp. boiled"

In the archaic language many words were derived from the principal parts of such strong verbs— either from the *ablaut* series (the specific series of vowels in the various forms: jó-ý-au-u-o) shown here, or from other systematically mutated versions of the stem vowels (by the process known as *umlaut*). These rules are fixed and only by their application can true etymologies be discovered. Just because a word looks or sounds like it *could be* related to another one, does not make it so unless the phonological rules fit *and* preferably a semantic corroboration can be established as well. An example of this from the Old Norse verb *sjóða* is provided by the word for "sheep," which is *sauðr*, derived from the past tense form of *sjóða*, *sauð*, "boiled," because sheep meat was most often boiled in its preparation for consumption. The linguistic world of etymology is a fascinating one that leads to the explanation of may mysteries, but the practice of pseudo-etymology leads only to misinformation and disinformation which causes one to become more stupid the more one absorbs it. The "occultizoid" world is full of such approaches.

Uses of *Seiðr* Reflected in the Historical Record

All examples of the use of the technique specifically identified in Old Norse sources as *seiðr* have been collected and translated by James A. Chisholm and Stephen E. Flowers. For those who want to consult the original texts, their book, noted in the bibliography of this book, is recommended.

A review of these texts reveals a great deal. It shows that *seiðr* is something other than Asiatic "shamanism," but that it is closely related to it in certain aspects. Such a review shows that there are very specific technical requirements for the practice of *seiðr*, which should not be ignored by would-be current revivers of the practices.

Technically, the practice of *seiðr* involves the production of vocal sounds, called *seiðlæti*. These sounds may be reconstructed from what can be heard of archaic survivals of sacred and/or magical vocal performances from the Eurasian geographical area, coupled with some empirical observation. Additionally, the performance of *seiðr* is most often carried out from a high, four-posted, platform, called a *seiðhjallr*.

Various accounts exist in the sagas concerning the nature of the *seiðhjallr* and its attendant practices. In the *Saga of Gísli* (ch. 11) we read that: "Now Thorgrímr hastened to the sorcery [*seiðr*] and looked to his equipment and made himself a scaffold [*hjallr*] and worked that magic [*fjölkyniliga*] with all its obscenity [*ergi*] and devilry [*skelmiskapr*]." A manuscript variant of this final passage reads: "And then Thorgrímr made himself a sorcery-platform [*seiðhjallr*] according to the custom that was usual there, and he put every exertion and strength [*kraptr*] into it." Elsewhere in chapter 35 of the *Laxdæla saga* we read that "Kotkell erected a large sorcery-platform [*seiðhjallr*] and they all climbed onto it. They sang hard-twisted knowledge [*frœði*] which were incantations [*galdrar*]. Soon there was a great storm." But perhaps the most dramatic image of the *seiðhjallr* is contained in the description of a magical battle with a sorceress named Skuld ("the greatest of magical-kind [*galdrakind*] and descended from elves [*af álfum*] on her mother's side") in chapter 32/33 of *Hrólf kraki's Saga*:

The queen Skuld did not work any tricks [bragð] while the bear was in King Hrólf's army, there she sat in her black tent on her sorcery-platform [í sínu svarta tjaldi á seiðhjalli sínum]. But things changed now as dim night follows bright day. King Hrólfr's men now saw a huge boar coming out of King Hjörvarðr's army: it was no smaller than an ox of three years age and was wolf-grey in color an arrow flew from each of his bristles, and in such a sinister fashion he felled King Hrólfr's soldiers in swathes.

Another dramatic account surrounding a seiðhjallr is found in the Friðþjólf's Saga (ch. 5) where we read about two sorceresses [seiðkonur], Heiðr and Hamgláma, hired to raise a magical storm against the hero and attack him at sea: "They worked the sorcery [efldu seiðinn], and ascended their platform [hjallr] with incantations [galdrar] and workings [gerningum]. . ." Friðþjólfr , however, sees the shape-shifting sorceresses on the back of a monstrous whale sent to attack his ship and says: "I see two women on the back of the whale, and they are causing this violent storm with their worst sorcery [seiðr] and incantations [galdrar]. Now we shall test which is greater: our luck [hamingja] or their witchcraft [trollskapr]." With great skill he struck the images of the seiðkonur with a forked pole and broke their backs. Later in the saga it is reported that " . . . when the two sisters were performing sorcery [váru at seiðnum] they fell from their sorcery-platform [seiðhjallr] and broke both their backs."

I would encourage everyone who is deeply interested to make their own review of the available material to synthesize his or her own view. The body of material is fairly small. It is found that the most general mistake made by people trying to reconstruct the seið-tradition is that they already have an idea of what they want the material to say and then they only read what they already "know" into that material. If one lets the material speak for itself, it will tell a wondrous tale.

Perhaps the most famous, and certainly the most extensive, text which reflects the sometimes complex technology of seiðr used for divinatory purposes is found in chapter 4 of the Saga of Erik the Red:

> At this very time there was a great famine in Greenland. Little was caught by those who went in search of game, some never came back. A woman named Thorbjorg was in the settlement.

She was a prophetess [*spákona*] and called the "Little Volva." She had nine sisters, all of whom were prophetesses [*spákonur*]. She was the only one left alive. It was Thorbjorg's custom to go to feasts in the winter, and people invited her to their homes most who wanted foreknowledge of their destiny [*forlög*] or that of the season. Because Thorkell was the leading freeholder, it was thought that he should find out when the hardship that afflicted them would stop. Thorkell bid the prophetess [*spákona*] to his dwelling and a good reception was made for her as was usual when this sort of a woman was received. A high-seat [*hásæti*] was prepared for her and a cushion in which there is supposed to be hen-feathers was set down. When she came in the evening with the man sent to escort her she was attired as follows: She wore a blue cloak with a strap. On the cloak were set precious stones down to the hem. She wore glass beads around her neck. She wore a black lambskin hood that was lined with cat-skin. In her hand she carried a staff [*stafr*] with a knob on it. It was decorated with brass and set with stones under the knob. She wore a touchwood belt and on it was a large skin-pouch in which she kept the talismans [*taufr*] that she needed for her magic [*fróðleikr*]. On her feet she wore hairy calf-skin shoes with long laces. There were large knobs of tin on the ends of the laces. On her hands she wore cat-skin gloves that were white and hairy on the inside.

When she arrived all thought they should give her a fit greeting, which she accepted according to her opinion of each person. Thorkell the farmer took the wise-woman [*vísendakona*] by the hand and led her to the seat which had been prepared for her. He asked her to cast her eyes over his home, household and hearth-fires. She had little to say about anything.

Tables were brought in around evening, and this is what the prophetess [*spákona*] had for her meal: she was given a gruel made from goat's milk, and the main dish of hearts from the various kinds of animals that were available there. She used a brass spoon, and a knife with a walrus-tusk handle bound with two rings of copper; the blade had a broken point.

When the tables had been removed Thorkell went over to Thorbjorg and asked her how she liked his home and people's behavior there, and how soon she would know the answer to his question which everyone wanted to learn. She replied that she would not give any answer until the following morning, when she slept there overnight first.

Late the next day she was supplied with the preparations she needed for performing the sorcery [*seiðr*]. She asked for the assistance of women who had knowledge [*fræði*] of the songs known as *Varðlokkur* which were needed to perform the sorcery [*seiðr*]. But no such women were available. Then they searched the farm to find out if anyone knew. Then Guðríð said: "I am neither magical [*fjölkunnig*] nor a wise-woman [*vísendakona*], but when I was in Iceland my foster-mother Halldís taught me the knowledge [*fræði*] which she called *Varðlokkur*. Thorbjorg said, "Then you are the person of knowledge [*fróðari*] I need." Then Guðríð said, "This is the kind of knowledge [*fræði*] and procedure [*atferli*] I want nothing to do with, because I am a Christian woman." "It may well be," said Thorbjorg, "that you could be of help to others over this, and not be any the worse a woman for that. But I shall leave it to Thorkell to provide whatever is required." Thorkell pressed Guðríð hard until she said she would do as he wished.

The women made a ring [*hringr*] around Thorbjorg who was seated up on the sorcery-platform [*seiðhjallr*]. Guðríð sang the song so beautifully and well that they were sure they had never heard lovelier singing. The prophetess [*spákona*] thanked her for the song [*kvæði*], and said that many spirits [*náttúrur*] had come to that place, which before had been turned from us and would grant us no obedience, as what had been sung seemed beautiful for them to hear. And now many things are revealed [*auðsýnir*] to me which were before hidden [*duldir*] from me and others. I can now say that the famine will not last much longer, and that conditions will improve with the spring; and the epidemic which has persisted for so long will abate sooner than expected. And as for you, Guðríð, I shall reward you at once for the help you have given us, for I can see your whole fate [*forlög*] with great clarity now. You will make a most distinguished marriage here in Greenland, but it will not last for long, for your paths all lead to Iceland; there you will start a great and eminent family line, and over your progeny there shall shine a bright light [*geisli*]. And now farewell my daughter."

Afterwards people went up to the wise-woman [*vísendakona*], each asking her whatever he was most curious to know. She answered them readily, and there were few things that did not turn out as she foretold. After this a messenger arrived from a neighboring farm and she went with him there. Then Thorbjörn was sent for; he refused to remain in the house while such heathenry [*heiðni*] was being practiced. (All of the major prophesies are said to have turned out.)

Another interesting passage of related type is found in chapter 11 of the more obscure *Nornagestsþáttr*. The hero of the saga, Gestr, comes to the court of king Óláfr Tryggvason of Norway and tells the king his life story which begins:

It was, when I was being brought up with my father in the place called Græning. My father was a rich man and maintained his dwelling-place in a fine manner. At that time sorceresses [*völvur*] were travelling around the countryside. They were called prophetesses [*spákonur*] and they prophesied [*spáðu*] men's fates [*aldr*]. Therefore people gave them lodgings and prepared feasts [*veizlur*] for them and gave them gifts upon their departure. My father did this too, and they came to his place with their entourage for them to prophesy [*spá*] my fate [*ørlög*]. I was still lying in the crib when they were supposed to speak about my case [*mál*]. There were two candle-lights burning above me. They spoke to me and said I would become a great man of luck [*auðnumaðr*] and more than my forebears or other noble sons there in the country and they said everything should go well for me in every respect. The youngest norn [*norn*] felt herself to have been neglected by the other two because they did not ask for her advice in such a prophesy [*spá*] of great value. Also there was a great crowd of

79

> rowdies there that knocked her from her seat [sæti] and she fell to the ground.
> Because of this she became fiercely angry. She then called out loudly and angrily and asked the others to cease such good utterances about me— "because I assign his fate [skapa] that he shall live no longer than that candle, which has been lit near the boy, burns."
> After this the oldest prophetess [völva] took the candle and put it out and asked my mother to keep sit and not to light it until it was the last day of my life. After this the prophetesses [spákonur] left and they bound the young norn [norn] and took her away as well, and my father gave them good gifts upon their departure. When I grew up my mother gave me this candle for safekeeping. I have it here with me now."
> The king said: "Why have you come here to us?"
> Gestr answered: "It just occurred to me. I expected there would be some lot of good fortune from you, because you have been praised to me by many good men and wise."

Of special interest here is the linkage between the divine Norns and the organization of human seeresses.

Besides prophecy, seiðr is used for a wide variety of magical purposes or motivations: to determine the condition of someone's ørlög, cause restlessness, cause storms or fog, influence the mental state of men and animals, prevent help from coming to someone, cause death or loss of luck, effect mind transfers, send a mara, cause sexual impotence, carry out reconnaissance, discover past events, or give cunning advice. Also frequently included among the possible uses of seiðr is shape-sifting (ON hamramr).

One interesting passage in the *Saga of Hákon the Good*(ch. 12) says that: ". . . by sorcery they put [létu síða] the intelligence [vit] of three men into the dog. He barked twice but spoke every third word." This description may provide a clue to the technology described elsewhere, for example in *Þiðreks saga af Bern*, where we read of a sorceress:

> We say that she went to practice sorcery [seiða], as was done in ancient times when magical women whom we call seeresses [völvur] would work sorcery [seiða (MS var. síða) seið]. So powerfully did she work magic [gerði hon af

> sér í fjölkyngi] and witchcraft [trollskapr] that she turned herself by sorcery [seiddi] into many kinds of animals: lions, bears and a great flying dragon... she herself was like a flying dragon.

The inner mechanics or technology of what is called *seiðr* is not a simple thing— it is a complex matter made up of several elements. The primary ingredient among these elements is, however, the induction of a trance state. This can be prolonged and profound, or it can come and go in a flash. *Seiðr* also frequently involves the aid of entities external to the *seið*-man or -woman. This is not unusual in the annals of magic— in fact it is more in keeping with the traditions of magic found in the rest of the world. Whereas *galdr* works from an ego-based, conscious center, *seiðr* works by means of consciousness being "tranced" into the external (objective) reality where it melds (if only momentarily) with substances and/or entities *external* to the ego-consciousness. In that state — or substantial matrix of the world — the unconscious will of the *seið*-man is able to work.

It is here that perhaps the essential technical link between *seiðr* and *wiccecræft* can be glimpsed. Whereas *galdr* is a will-based magical technology, *seiðr* and *wiccecræft* represent a trance-based magical technique. The roots of the distinction are found in the structural meanings of Óðinn's two hypostatic brothers: Vili and Vé: Will and Sacrality. Vé refers to something *separate from* the normal or ordinary. When viewed from the perspective of *mental states* this *vé*-condition is tantamount to the trance-state— a state of mind wholly other than, and separate from, ordinary consciousness. This state of mind can then be utilized in order to make changes in the world, and thus a form of magic is created. This, by the way, lends more semantic credence to the etymology of the word *wicce* which connects it to the root *weik- > *wīh-: 'holy.' (See my article on the holy in *Green Rûna*.)

Appendix A

Witchcraft and Runecraft: Two Different Paths

The Germanic magical traditions have been re-emerging slowly over the past century. The pace of the revival quickened with the rebirth of witchcraft, but there has been some confusion over the exact and authentic nature of what is being revived. It is our opinion that the more authentic and genuine the roots of a thing are, the stronger will be its trunk and the sweeter its fruits. True witchcraft needs to be given a chance to show what it can be in its own right, free of encumbering elements. There has, for example, been the constant effort of those who would revive an English, Norse or otherwise Germanic "wicca" to put Óðinn/Wôden in a prominent place, and to make use of the runes in their magical technology somehow. This is understandable. Once one is in the grip of the sometimes grim, but always overwhelmingly powerful All-Father and his runic array of magical arts it may be difficult to see anything else. At the same time there has been confusion as Vanic elements or attitudes particular to true witchcraft have often diluted the necessary precision and intellectual rigor of the Odinic path. In ancient times rune-galdor and witchcraft were technically two separate and distinct paths. Individuals and groups may have sought to master both— but this did not dilute or obscure the distinction between them. That there is today a general lack of discrimination and knowledge concerning these two traditional esoteric "schools" of the ancient North is perhaps a leading factor preventing these traditions from reaching their full potential. In this appendix we want to show the original *diversity* of the old ways and to promote an authentically pluralistic approach to these traditions today.

The old *Vanatrú* (Vana-Troth) and *Ásatrú* (Asa-Troth) were bound together in a common greater Troth, or religious system which encompassed all the Gods and Goddesses of the Germanic pantheon. This system held a general theology, cosmology and set of ethical values in common. This is what made them all "true" — or *loyal* — to the ancestral tradition.

A Book of Troth is an attempt to reach that level of commonality— it is intended equally to please and challenge the reader to arrive at a new balance from within under the sign of the hammer.

The situation with the common religion or Greater Troth as compared to the particular "sects" or schools within it can be compared to the way Hinduism works. Sects within Hinduism may differ widely on practice and the particulars of their philosophies— ranging from a kind of "philosophical atheism" (the *samkhya* system or philosophy) to a sort of "fundamentalism" (most common with the worshippers of Vishnu or Krishna)— but what they all hold in common are things such as belief in the infallibility of the *Veda*, reincarnation, immortality of the soul, a doctrine of *karma* (result of action), and the doctrine of the three *gunas*. It is principally on the first of these that Buddhists part with Hindus— and for that reason (and because they insist on proselytizing) they could not fit into Indian society.

Within the greater troth there is really no room for ideas such as "heresy." As originally conceived the troth is defined as those who acknowledge the Germanic pantheon as their own (to which they are connected by blood and/or choice) who in some way acknowledge and observe the holy days of the Germanic calendar (preferably *at least* three times a year in rites involving all the Gods and Goddesses in common), and who acknowledge the *Poetic Edda* as the primary source-work of spiritual and religious values. This latter point does not mean that the *Edda* is considered "holy writ" in the sense Jews, Christians, Muslims, Zoroastrians and others have a body of canonized texts. In the troth the attitude is all-inclusive— nothing is excluded or rejected as a source. But the sources are nevertheless *ranked in value.*

Beyond the Greater Troth, and probably closer to the hearts of individuals, are the individual schools, gilds, and bands devoted to one deity, group of deities, or idea. An example of one of these devoted to Wôden/Óðinn would be the Rune-Gild. Just as witchdom is devoted to the Lord and Lady. Both witchdom and the Rune-Gild are interested in magic, of course, and it might be interesting to note how these two approaches — both in ancient and modern times — differ from one another. In exploring these differences you will be able to get a feel for the differences between the truly Odian and the truly Vanic approach to things.

The Vanic way is dedicated to the Lord and Lady, while the Rune-Gild focuses on Óðinn (and secondarily on Freyja). True witches *worship* the Lord and Lady (especially the divinity of the sex opposite to their own), while runemasters pattern their own initiatory development after the model provided by Óðinn (or Freyja). The Vanic way is intuitive and sensual in its orientation, while the Runic way is *rationally* intuitive and "intellectual" in its orientation. Vana-Troth is rather syncretic around the edges and thus elements from non-Germanic cultures seem to mix in more easily. With the Runic way, foreign influences are first completely digested and reconfigured before they are accepted as a part of the tradition. Nowhere is this process clearer than with the Runes themselves. In ancient times the Odinic Erulians completely reformed and re-configured the Greco-Italic-Etruscan writing system according to their inner model. Only *then* could it become part of their rational and analytic system. More typical of the Vanic approach would be the intuitive collection and use of holy signs and symbols in orders and systems created spontaneously. In other words, writers on the runes such as R. Blum, P. M. H. Atwater and most others are trying to apply a Vanic approach to the Æsiric topic of the Runes. The mixture has not been as fruitful as a more aware approach might have offered. Many people who have been attracted to the Germanic system, and who have instantly gravitated toward the Runes (sometimes because they seemed to be the only coherent magical system in the tradition) would perhaps be better served by taking the Vanic approach and putting the Fuþark aside. The Vanic way is that of the person close to nature and to the senses, while the Odian way is that of the person close to the transcendental laws of the cosmos and psyche (human intellect).

Besides all the things which separate the two systems, of course, there are hidden affinities between Freyja and Óðinn. This relationship in the divine world is a reflection of, and is reflected in, the hidden links between members of esoteric schools dedicated to these two deities.

Óðinn as the chief sovereign God of the Germanic peoples, is a God who specializes in *synthesizing opposites*. As such he is an ideal model for an "Imperial God," i.e. one who expands his fields of rulership to take in the realms of other divinities. *Working from above* he becomes a God of warriors, and a God of wealth, pleasure and production. He synthesizes the functions of Þórr and of the Vanir. This is who and how all of the elder faith could come to be understood as "Odinism." By the same token the Vanadís, not to be outdone, expands her fields of rulership *working from below*. She, as primarily a Goddess of wealth, pleasure and production, takes in a warrior function and comes to be considered a sovereign queen—Freyja: the (Royal) Lady. These two tendencies should not be understood in *historical terms*— they are intrinsic and innate in the essences of the two divinities. They did not "develop" these traits over time, but rather they were in them in seed-form from the beginning.

For those who know the code, the different ways in which Óðinn and Freyja work is as follows: Óðinn works vertically, Freyja works horizontally.

From the standpoint of the Odian Rune-Gild it can be said that Vanic studies and experience in the realm of *seiðr* and *wiccecræft* is serious and ongoing. This book is in fact a by-product of that effort. It is, however, also expected that an independent esoteric school primarily dedicated to the Vana-Troth and to the operative techniques of *seiðr* or witchcraft will develop as a parallel to the Rune-Gild. The genuineness of this alternative school will be judged by how well the Rune-Gild and it can cooperate. In ancient times the spirit of cooperation was strong, while at the same time each was fully independent of the other.

It might be said again, although the analogy only goes so far, that the Vana-Troth is similar to Tantrism (*tantra yoga*) and the Asa-Troth is akin to Vedism (or *raja yoga* or *jñāna yoga* or *mantra yoga*) in India. This analogy tends to break down (as do the Indian distinctions) the deeper one goes into the esoteric levels of the two schools. At their deepest levels of reality and at their highest levels of personal initiation the two schools have much more in common. But ultimately their outer differences mirror an inner distinction: the Vana-Troth aims for final union with the forces of nature, while the Rune-Master aims for eternal individuation from the cosmic order in fellowship with Óðinn in Valhöll. Both paths are noble, both are worthy. It is just a matter of finding the one that is right for you.

Appendix B

Ásatrú and Vanatrú

The relationship between the two major branches of the ancient Germanic religion — the Asa-Troth and the Vana-Troth — is one fraught with mythic and apparent *conflict*. In ancient times this conflict was fully resolved. That is essentially the story as reflected in Germanic myth— but it is a resolution which does not reduce the two groups to clones of each other. The dichotomy inherent in the powers represented by the Æsir and Vanir learn to cooperate, without losing their identity one to the other. Such a relationship-model has become increasingly foreign to us in a modern world obsessed with making everyone the same. The polar dichotomy of the Æsir and Vanir is something which is inherent, and which needs to be preserved and respected.

Therefore we are faced with an essential and ancient dichotomy. The first dichotomy— the First War, or conflict between the Æsiric and Vanic powers is a given. Nothing we can do can change this— nor should anyone try. We should follow the wise example outlined in the Norse tradition itself and synthesize these powers. Atavistic conflicts and frictions will arise, but they can be resynthesized repeatedly.

Perfect harmony between the Ásatrú and Vanatrú would be a sure sign of the death of the powers in question. The fact that when brought together — even today — there is an intrinsic tension, and even conflict, is a sign of the continuing *vitality* of the powers. What is needed is mutual respect and recognition of differences in spiritual approaches. As in the Germanic cosmology in general, once *two* exists, then an infinite number of other possibilities arise.

The source of the dichotomy lies in the essential differences between the functions of the Æsir and Vanir. The Æsir divide and discriminate between "this" and "that," they use verbal symbols to transcend the ordinary boundaries of perception, consciously synthesize opposites and use physical force to defend and expand their vision. These activities describe the workings of the first two functions of the pantheon. The Vanic third function operates differently. The Vanir begin with an assumption of wholeness. However, an intrinsic duality is necessary to their chief function — production and reproduction of themselves. This organic basis is essentially rooted in sexuality. The basis of their power is organic and material. The sovereign power they wield is based on economic vitality, not on ideas of justice or raw physical power (two roots of Æsiric sovereign power).

In ancient times, without being dogmatic or doctrinaire about it, the folk made use of the entire array of spiritual powers available to them in the pantheon. Certain tribes at certain times would gravitate toward one or the other parts of the pantheon as social, political, military or economic conditions dictated. But the whole of the system was available at all times.

This sense of mutual interdependence between and among the various parts of the complex Germanic pantheon is a spirit which must return to the folk as a part of the true reawakening of our eternal native spirituality. The trick will be in cooperating without "selling out." The modern (crypto-Christian) model would reduce the Vanir to the Æsir or the other way around. The true model is more difficult to grasp: that the Vanir remain the Vanir, and the Æsir remain who they are, but that they, despite their differences, work in a cooperative fashion for the benefit of the whole folk. The maintenance of the distinction between these two forces is actually a source of energy and vitality in the system, and additionally acts as an insurance against creeping monotheism—the root of all totalitarianisms.

Appendix C
Ásatrú and Modern "Wicca"

Historically there has been an extremely ambivalent relationship between many members of the revived Ásatrú groups and modern "Wiccans." This springs from a number of sources, ranging from personal rivalries to general style and aesthetics. But the deep underlying source of the ambivalence is that Ásatrú – or the Troth – has valued hard scholarship from its inception– an inception which actually lies back in the Romantic Period of European history. This is in decided contrast to the increasingly free-form attitude prevalent in the practice of modern "Wicca."

As a matter of fact it seems to me that the best elements of modern "Wicca" have been evolving back into the Vana-Troth. Typically, members of the Ásatrú world often seem impatient with the speed of this evolution. All one has to do is mention the word "Wicca" in a room full of Ásatrúarfolk and one will be bombarded with a flurry of usually negative opinions and mutterings about the dangers of "Wicca-trú." I have found that one of the main reasons for this is that those holding these strong opinions are as often as not "ex-Wiccans" who will, if you get to know them, tell you stories of how they became disillusioned with modern Wicca after they were mistreated at the hands of some manipulative "queen-bee" High Priestess or "witch-master" High Priest in their youth.

Sociologists who study "neo-pagan" and other alternative religious movements have noted that the typical (average) length of interest in such things is about four and a half years. After that the individual either returns to more mainstream traditions or gives up altogether any "spiritual quest." I see the main *reasons* for this as two: 1) rampant eclecticism– what is called in the Rune-Gild tradition the "Path of the Squirrel"— and 2) the general vacuousness of the "neo-pagan traditions." A genuine historical tradition based on reality, with deep roots along with both tradition and spirituality is what is needed to counteract the four and a half year "burn-out."

A true tradition cannot pander to the aspirants' market-driven appetite for a new intellectual bauble to play with every so often. The aspirant must have faith in the trueness of the tradition, based on its genuineness. In the case of the Germanic tradition, of course, its genuineness is not in question: The very fact that we still use the old Germanic names for our weekday names: Tuesday, Wednesday, Thursday, Friday— speaks to how deeply ingrained and natural *this* particular heathen tradition is in our own culture. This genuine base of knowledge and eternal depth of material is what Ásatrú and Vanatrú *can* provide to the "neo-pagan" world of today. This authenticity is the only effective counter-balance to the insidious eclecticism and traditional emptiness which haunts modern "neo-paganism" most exemplified by modern Wicca. Authenticity thwarts in a positive way the machinations of shallow and pompous "High Priestesses" by requiring knowledge of an organic body lore which cannot be exhausted. Eclecticism is vanquished and the traditional vacuum filled with the mysterious depth of an organic system of thought which is natural to the aspirant. It is this spirit of innate tradition, opposed to the arbitrary and inorganic eclecticism of modern Wicca which sets Ásatrú against modern "Wicca" on a visceral level. In the future it will be more likely that those who follow a "pagan" path will gravitate more and more to paths which are in fact organic and natural to *them* as organic beings. When this happens the marketing spell of eclecticism will loose its charm and the differences between the organic Ásatrú groups and the (formerly) eclectic Wiccans will fade.

Appendix D

Traditional Witchdom and Modern Wicca

This book is bound to raise a good deal of controversy. This stems from a variety of conflicts which are handled in these appendices. Here the topic of the relationship between the modern religion of "Wicca" and the traditional patterns of ancient Witchdom are discussed, and it is hoped, a meeting point discovered whereby a dialog can be created between traditional Witchdom and modern Wicca.

In many respects modern Wicca seems to be a pale reflection of traditional witchdom. Gerald Gardner and his cohorts were far too influenced by medieval ceremonial magic to be able to view the sources of *wiccecræft* precisely. (Many or Gardner's descriptions of ritual tools were taken directly from the *Key of Solomon*, for example.) This is not to say that over the centuries between the period of medieval Christianization and the 20th century such a syncretism could not have actually taken place. But the philosophy followed by traditional witchdom is one which exhorts us to return to the well-springs of knowledge for the regular renewal of the lore. Our intellectual tools are constantly getting better. It is our responsibility to *use* them, and use them *wisely*.

Curiously, it is the very elements for which Gardnerianism is often criticized — even among "Gardnerians" — which were probably the most traditional from an operative angle. Elements such as binding the initiate and flagellating him or her as a part of the ceremony are probably among the oldest and most genuine elements of the working formula— yet they tend to be the very features which are the first to be rejected in the progressive *modernization* of "the craft."

As outlined in earlier parts of this book, the word "Wicca," and much of the lore surrounding it, are genuine insofar as they are drawn from the Anglo-Saxon and Norse heritage of the English countryside. What was being glimpsed by the earlier practitioners of modern Wicca was indeed the old Vana-Troth. This is the true *wiccan* heritage to which it is destined, at least in part, to return.

Traditional Vana-Troth, or Witchdom, is characterized by a focus on *tradition*. That is, a connection between objective aspects of lore from the past and contemporary practice. Also included in the definition of what it means to be *traditional* is an understanding that the essence of the religious system is tied up with a natural approach, which includes tribalism and the idea that the Gods and Goddesses of the Troth are ingrained in the very blood and bones of the adherents. Traditional religion is not a matter of "choice"— you are what you are, and your divinities are what they are. This reality can be denied, but it can not be invalidated.

However, Vana-Troth is much more oriented toward an intuitive and "feeling" approach than is Asa-Troth, or *Ásatrú*. Whereas the Asa-Troth may rely on 70 percent objective knowledge as a basis for intuitive explorations and experience, which accounts for the other 30 percent, with the Vana-Troth this approximate ratio is reversed.

The Vana-Troth is also more a local phenomenon. It is not so much fostered by webpages, newsletters and long-distance communication, but rather is a matter of real people getting together on a local basis— creating a family or tribe.

Modern Wicca is a product of a certain time, place and culture— the mid 20th century in southern England among members of the "occult underground." It was born of an ingenious insight and based on a powerful set of working techniques. However, in subsequent years the Wiccan apparatus degenerated into a political tool for the advancement of "multi-culturalism" and other neo-Marxist ideologies. This stems from the fact that traditional Witchdom was and is a tool for the continuation of timeless tradition, whereas modern Wicca is a religious system born of a time when such traditions were being broken down and discarded. Modern Wicca embraces an inorganic dualism. An example of this is that although the God and Goddess may be worshipped, and "male" and "female" principles acknowledged in the abstract, true to form as a *modern* ideology these abstract principles are not *necessarily* linked to real live human bodies. This would have been unthinkable to our ancestors who thought of this world as a wonderful place, and who wanted to continue their eternal tribal life within it.

Another essential aspect of modern Wicca entirely foreign to traditional religion is its reductionism. "Everything is everything else, all things are equal and the same at some level." This attitude is not an attempt to express the mystical state at the end of a long journey, but rather is a dogmatic approach to the beginning of the journey. This kind of approach is linked to a cult of eclecticism which celebrates a lack of discernment and discrimination. One of the chief problems this may cause in the development of individuals is that there is no traditional ballast for the ship which is the individual. If all things are in all ways at all times equal, then what's the point?

Perhaps Wicca fell victim to the modern "occult market." If the market extoled the virtues of purity and intensity of focus on one's path then it would be very difficult to make the "seeker" believe he or she needed to delve into Tarot, astrology, Runes, Wicca, the Golden Dawn, Egyptian magic, Greek mythology, *I Ching*, and so forth *ad infinitum*. After exploring all these alternatives for a few years the average seeker will quit altogether or go back to more socially acceptable forms of spirituality. It is the rampant eclecticism which is the essential problem here. With a focused traditional approach, rather than a scattered modern eclectic approach, the seeker should have just gotten the basics down enough to really start the journey after four years. Instead the "occult journeyman" is ready to give up because the implicit promise of dramatic and exciting change offered by a procession of schools and techniques has fallen short. The bloom of early spiritual romance fading after just a few months in each instance. In some cases this is because the very system being explored has not even been endowed with the age-old depth that can only come in connection with an objective traditional system. If a system has been invented as a work of art and its essential components cannot be verified transpersonally in conjunction with a genuine and authentic *mythology* (i.e. matrix of meaningful patterns) then it is bound to fall short of the mark eventually. This is where many Wiccans and ex-Wiccan find themselves today.

The Vana-Troth or the Witchdom of the True can bridge this gap. By being a system which *is* based on traditional, verifiable and objective transpersonal models of mythology and archetypes the Vana-Troth can now begin to establish new rings or bands of worshippers based on these inherent and innate patterns. Not only can new rings be started, but old "covens" of modern Wiccans can and have begun to "convert" to the Vana-Troth, or true (i.e. *loyal*) "Wicca."

The action which now must be taken is manifold. There is a vast amount of research and development which waits to be done in the context of the Vana-Troth. There is a vast sea of information waiting to be explored— most efforts up to this point have only opened doors but few have stepped very far into the rooms beyond those doors. One of the most exciting things about this journey is that those who choose to undertake it will transcend the "occult underground" culture, and will not have to hide their heads in shame when in the presence of intellectual masters of the lore as one might find at a university or college. This has been the bane of the "occult subculture" over the past century or more. It is time once more to step forward into the serious intellectual life of our own cultures and not hide in the shadows anymore. Part of doing this requires that those interested in the reawakening of the Vana-Troth begin to *network* with each other around the world. Communication organs on the internet as well as more conventional means must be developed as a prelude to the widespread re-establishment of rings or bands of the Vana-True around the world.

The Vana-Troth, or the Witchdom of the True, need not be in an antagonistic relationship to the modern practice of Wicca. In many ways the modern religion seems to have been largely drawn or derived from the archetypes of the ancient cult of the Lord and Lady as practiced in Scandinivized England of the early Middle Ages. Therefore a great deal of information can be derived from this culture which can enrich the lore of the modern cult. The call of the Vana-Troth is, however, one which exhorts its followers to return to authentic roots which can be verified objectively and to return to the traditional ideas of tribal, blood-linked, religion and away from the universalist (Christian-derived) idea that "religion" is a matter of arbitrary and individual choice— like what kind of car to buy.

Notes

(1) H.R. Davidson, "Folklore and man's past." *Folklore* 74 (1963), p. 535.

(2) For a brief discussion of the revival of the Germanic tradition, see chapter 4 of my *Runelore*, but for a more thorough discussion see my *The Northern Dawn*, to be published by Rûna-Raven in 2000.

(3) For a brief discussion of the Celtic revival see chapter 2 of Tadhg MacCrossan's *The Sacred Cauldron* (St. Paul, MN: Llewellyn, 1991). This book is unfortunately no longer in print. We await a comprehensive treatment of the Celtic revival.

(4) For a down-to-earth discussion of some of the fanciful aspects of the witchcraft phenomenon, see Elliot Rose, *Razor for a Goat* (Toronto: University of Toronto Press, 1989).

(5) Valiente, *The Rebirth of Witchcraft*, p. 32

(6) John Hargrave *The Confession of the Kibbo Kift* (London: Duckworth, 1927), p. 55.

(7) For an interesting discussion of the connections between the Woodcraft movement and modern Wicca, see the article "The Red God: Woodcraft and the Origins of Wicca." by J. Greer and Gordon Cooper in *Gnosis* 48 (Summer, 1998), pp. 50-58.

(8) For a comprehensive collection of texts referring to *seiðr*, see Chisholm and Flowers' *A Source-Book of Seið* (Smithville: The Rune-Gild, 1998).

(9) See Ibn Fadlan, *Ibn Fadlan's Travel-Report as it concerns the Scandinavian Rûs*, p. 11, and the commentary by Stephen Flowers on p. 20.

Glossary

Æsir, sg. *Áss*: The Gods and Goddesses in the Germanic pantheon which govern the powers of sovereignty and physical force.

Anglo-Saxon: The culture and language of the Germanic invaders of Britain who established their culture following 450 CE. Also often used generally as a synonym for Old English, the language spoken in England between 450 and approximately 1100 CE.

Ásgarðr: The enclosure of the Gods, the realm where the Gods and Goddesses exist. (ON Ásgarðr)

blessing: The act of sacrificing and distributing the powers of the Gods and Goddesses in Midgard. (OE *bletsian*, to sacrifice)

dis, pl. dises: Ancestral female divinities to whom Winter Nights and Disting are holy. (ON *dís; dísir*)

earth: 1) The natural, physical aspects of the universe, 2) The planet Earth, 3) soil.

English: The language and culture of the Germanic peoples who began to settle in the British Isles around 450 CE and the subsequent developments of that language and culture.

etin: A "giant," which is a living entity of great age and strength, and often knowledge. (ON *jötunn; jötnar*)

fetch: A numinous being attached to every individual, which is the repository of all past action and which accordingly affects the person's life: the personal divinity. (ON *fylgja*)

folk: 1) The Teutonic or Germanic nation (all people of Teutonic heritage, German, English, Dutch, Scandinavian, etc.), 2) The people gathered for a holy event.

frith: The true Germanic word for "peace" which carries with it the implication of "freedom."

galdor: 1) A magical incantation or mantra. 2) A form of magic which often uses runestaves as a method of objectifying verbal contents and thus objectify magical intent. (ON *galdr*, pl. *galdrar*)

Germanic: The language and culture of a group of Indo-European people who became a distinct linguistic and cultural group in the vicinity of southern Sweden and northern Germany sometime in the first millennium BCE and who, over time and space, gave rise to the German, Dutch and Scandinavian (Danish, Swedish, Norwegian and Icelandic), and Anglo-Saxon, or English, languages and cultures.

harrow: 1) An outdoor altar usually made of stone, 2) A general term of the altar in a true working. (OE *hearg*, ON *hörg*)

heathen: Originally meaning "someone or something from the countryside," or "heath," it came to designate the pre-Christian culture, as Christianity was initially an urban phenomenon.

holy: There are two aspects to this term: 1) that which is filled with divine power, and 2) that which is marked off and separate from the profane.

lore: The tradition in all its aspects.

Middlert: the dwelling place of humanity, the physical plane of existence. Also, called Midgard or Mid-yard, the enclosure in the midst of all. (OE Middangeard, ON *Miðgarðr*).

multiverse: The many states of being (worlds) that make up the universe. Used when focusing on the multiplicity of being.

norn: One of the three female wights who embody the process of cause and effect and evolutionary force.

ørlög: ON Literally analyzed this means "primal layers" (primal laws)— the past action of an individual or the cosmos) that shapes present reality, and that which should come about as a result of it. Its root concept is the same as English wyrd or weird.

ragnarök: ON Literally this means the "judgment of the Gods," it is an end of a cycle of existence, great or small.

seiðr: A kind of magical technique contrasted with galdor. *Seiðr* involves attaining of trance states and often involves sexuality. Sometimes this involves shape-shifting into animal forms. Typically it is performed by volvas who would roam the countryside and attend feasts where they would sit on a wooden platform and with the aid of the magical songs of their assistants they could obtain visions of the future. It is the kind of magic taught to Óðinn by Freyja.

soul: 1) A general term for the psychic parts of the psycho-physical complex, 2) The postmortem shade. (OE *sáwl*)

thurs: A strong kind of giant embodying great cosmic forces but devoid of intelligence.

tide: A time, occasion, a span of time with a definite beginning and end. Example: Yule-tide.

troth: Religion, being loyal to the Gods and Goddesses and cultural values of the ancestors. (ON *trú*, OE *treowþ*)

true: Adjectival form of "troth," can mean "loyal." A "true man" is a man loyal to the Gods and Goddesses of his ancestors, and "true wicca" means a form of witchcraft which is loyal to the ancestral Gods and Goddesses worshipped by those who first used *wiccecræft*.

Vanir, sg. **Van:** ON The Gods and Goddesses of organic existence in the Germanic pantheon, governing the realms of organic and material production and reproduction, eroticism, wealth, craftsmanship and physical well-being. The modern English form would be: Wane(s).

vé: ON An outdoor sacred enclosure open to the sky.

völva: A female magician who specializes in *seiðr* magic.

Wane(s): See Vanir.

Wicca/n: A modern neo-pagan religion practiced according to an eclectic formula

wicca/n: A term that has been butchered among neo-pagans. *Wicca* is an Old English (Anglo-Saxon) word for a male sorcerer. The possessive case of this word grammatically is *wiccan*— which would translate to "witch's." So when we say "the wiccan year," we can understand it grammatically as the "witch's year, or the year as understood by the practitioner of *wiccecræft*.

wight: A being or entity of any kind with some independent living or conscious quality.

worship: Literally this means simply "to give honor (worth) to something— and that is all that it means in the terminology of the Vana-Troth.

world: The psycho-chronic human aspects of the manifested universe. (OE *weoruld,* the age of a man.) The cosmos.

World-Tree, see Yggdrasill.

wyrd: The process of the unseen web of synchronicity and cause and effect throughout the cosmos. Same as weird.

Yggdrasill: The framework of the cosmos which supports the nine major realms or worlds.

Bibliography

Bauschatz, Paul C. *The Well and the Tree: World and Time in Early Germanic Culture.* Amherst: University of Massachusetts Press, 1982.
Buchholz, Peter. "Schamanistische Züge in der altisländischen Überlieferung." Diss. Münster University, 1968.
Chaney, William A. *The Cult of Kingship in Anglo-Saxon England: The Transition from Paganism to Christianity.* Berkeley, CA: University of California Press, 1970.
Chisholm, James. *True Hearth.* Smithville, Texas: Rûna-Raven Press, 1994.
Chisholm, James A. and Stephen E. Flowers, eds. and trs. *A Source-Book of Seiðr: The Corpus of Old Icelandic Texts Dealing with Seiðr and Related Words.* Smithville: The Rune-Gild, 1998.
Cleasby, Richard and Gudbrand Vigfusson. *An Icelandic-English Dictionary.* Oxford: At the Clarendon Press, 1957, 2nd ed.
Davidson, Hilda R. (Ellis). *The Road to Hel.* Cambridge: Cambridge University Press, 1943.
Davidson, H. R. Ellis. "Hostile Magic in the Icelandic Sagas." In: *The Witch Figure* Ed. V. Newell. Boston and London: Routledge and Kegan Paul, 1973, pp. 20-41.
——————. *Gods and Myths of Northern Europe.* Harmondsworth: Penguin, 1964.
——————. *Roles of the Northern Goddess.*
Dumézil, Georges. *The Destiny of a Warrior.* tr. A. Hiltebeitel. Chicago: University of Chicago Press, 1970.
——————. *From Myth to Fiction: The Saga of Hadingus.* tr. D. Coltman. Chicago: University of Chicago Press, 1973.
——————. *Gods of the Ancient Northmen.* E. Haugen, ed. Berkeley: University of California Press, 1973.
Fadlan, Ibn. *Ibn Fadlan's Travel-Report as it concerns the Scandinavian Rûs.* Ed. Stephen E. Flowers. Smithville, Texas: Rûna-Raven, 1998.
Gardner, Gerald. *Witchcraft Today.* London: Rider, 1954.
Gardner, Gerald. *The Meaning of Witchcraft.* London: Aquarian, 1959.

Gaster, Theodor H. *The New Golden Bough: A New Abridgement of the Classic Work by James Frazer.* New York: S. G. Phillips, 1959.

Greer, John Michael and Gordon Cooper. "The Red God: Woodcraft and the Origins of Wicca." *Gnosis* 48 (Summer, 1998), 50-58.

Grimm, Jacob. *Teutonic Mythology.* tr. S. Stallybrass. New York: Dover, 1966, 4 vols.

Grønbech, Vilhelm. *The Culture of the Teutons.* London: Oxford University Press, 1931, 2 vols.

Gurevich, Aron. *Medieval Popular Culture: Problems of Belief and Perception.* Cambridge: Cambridge University Press, 1988.

Hollander, Lee M., tr. *The Poetic Edda.* Austin: University of Texas Press, 1962, 2nd ed.

Ingham, Marion. *The Goddess Freyja and Other Female Figures in Germanic Mythology and Folklore.* Diss. Cornell University, 1985.

Jones, Gwyn. *A History of the Vikings.* London: Oxford University Press, 1984, 2nd ed.

——————, tr. *Erik the Red and other Icelandic Sagas.* Oxford: Oxford University Press, 1961.

Kelcher, Georgia Dunham. *Dreams in Old Norse Literature and their Affinities in Folklore.* Cambridge: Cambridge University Press, 1935.

Kelly, Aiden. *Crafting the Art of Magic.* St. Paul, MN: Llewellyn, 1991.

Knightly, Charles. *The Customs and Ceremonies of Britain: An Encyclopaedia of Living Traditions with a Calendar of Customs and a Regional Gazetter.* London: Thames and Hudson, 1986.

Näsström, Britt-Mari. *Freyja- the Great Goddess of the North.* (= Lund Studies in History of Religion vol 5) Lund: Almquist & Wiksell, 1995.

Pálsson, Hermann and Edwards, Paul, trs. and ed. *Seven Viking Romances.* Harmondsworth: Penguin, 1985.

Polomé, Edgar. "Freyja." *Reallexikon der germanischen Altertumskunde* 9 (1995), pp. 584-587.

——————. "Freyr." *Reallexikon der germanischen Altertumskunde* 9 (1995), pp. 587-594.

Pulsiano, Phillip, et al. eds. *Medieval Scandinavia: An Encyclopedia.* New York: Garland, 1993.

Renfrew, Colin. *Archaeology and Language: The Puzzle of Indo-European Origins.* Cambridge: Cambridge University Press, 1988.

Rose, Elliot. *Razor for a Goat.* Toronto: University of Toronto Press, 1989.

Russell, James C. *The Germanization of Early Medieval Christianity: A Sociohistorical Approach to Religious Transformation.* Oxford: Oxford University Press, 1994.

Simpson, Jacqueline. *Everyday Life in the Viking Age.* New York: Dorset Press, 1967.

Strömbäck, Dag. *Sejd: Textstudier i nordisk religionshistoria* (= Nordiska texter och undersökningar 5) Stockholm: Gerber, 1935.

Sturluson, Snorri. *The Prose Edda.* Tr. A. Brodeur. New York: American Scandinavian Foundation, 1929.

Thorsson, Edred. *Runelore.* York Beach, ME: Weiser, 1986.

——————. *A Book of Troth.* St. Paul, MN: Llewellyn, 1989.

——————. *Green Rûna: The Runemasters Notebook: Shorter Works of Edred Thorsson. Volume I.* Smithville, Texas: Rûna-Raven Press, 1996.

Turville-Petre, E.O.G. *Myth and Religion of the North.* New York: Holt, Rinehart and Winston, 1964.

Valiente, Doreen. *The Rebirth of Witchcraft.* Custer, WA: Phoenix. 1989.

Vries, Jan de. *Altgermanische Religionsgeschichte.* Berlin: de Gruyter, 1956-57, 2 vols.

——————. *Altnordisches etymologisches Wörterbuch.* Leiden: Brill, 1961.

Webb, James. *The Occult Establishment.* La Salle, IL: Open Court, 1976.

Williams, Mary. *Social Scandinavia in the Viking Age.* New York: MacMillan, 1930.

Map I: Vanic Deity Sites

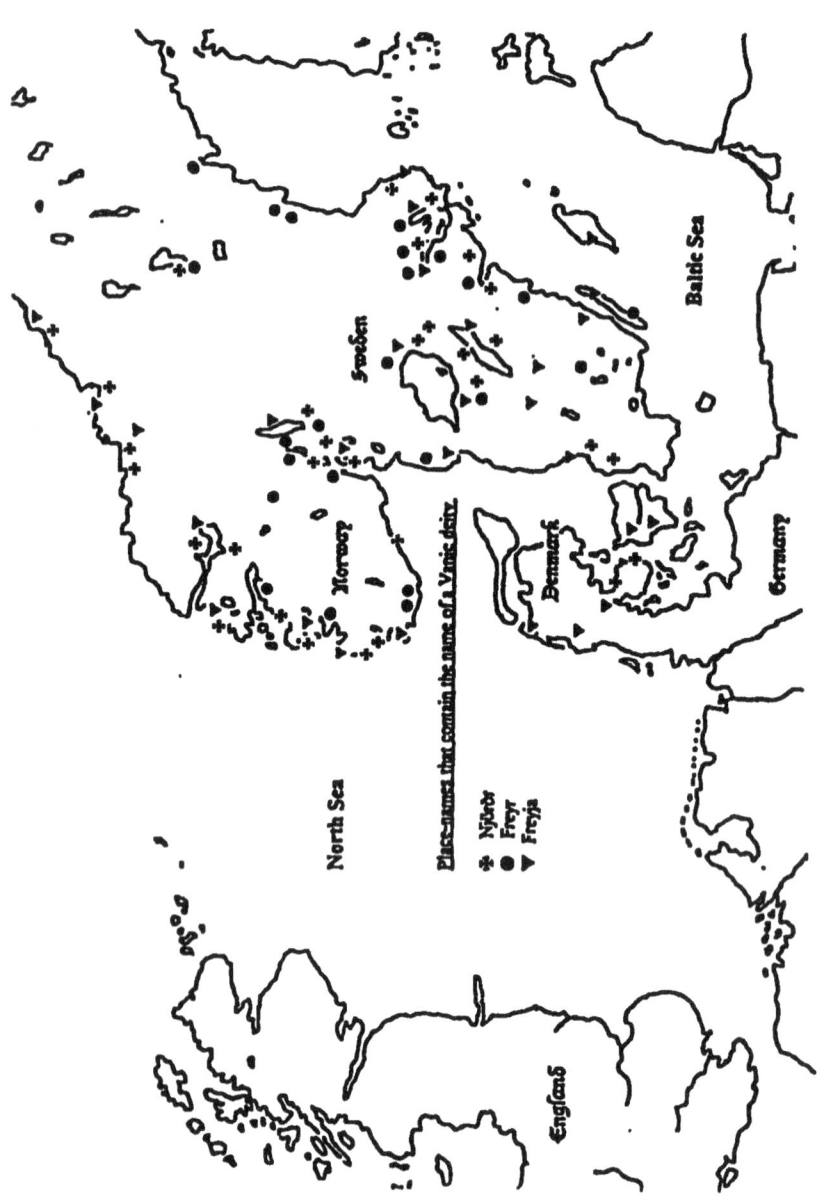

Map II: Heptarchy of Anglo-Saxon England and the Danelaw

Map III: The Cult Sites of Freyja

Map IV: The Cult Sites of Freyr

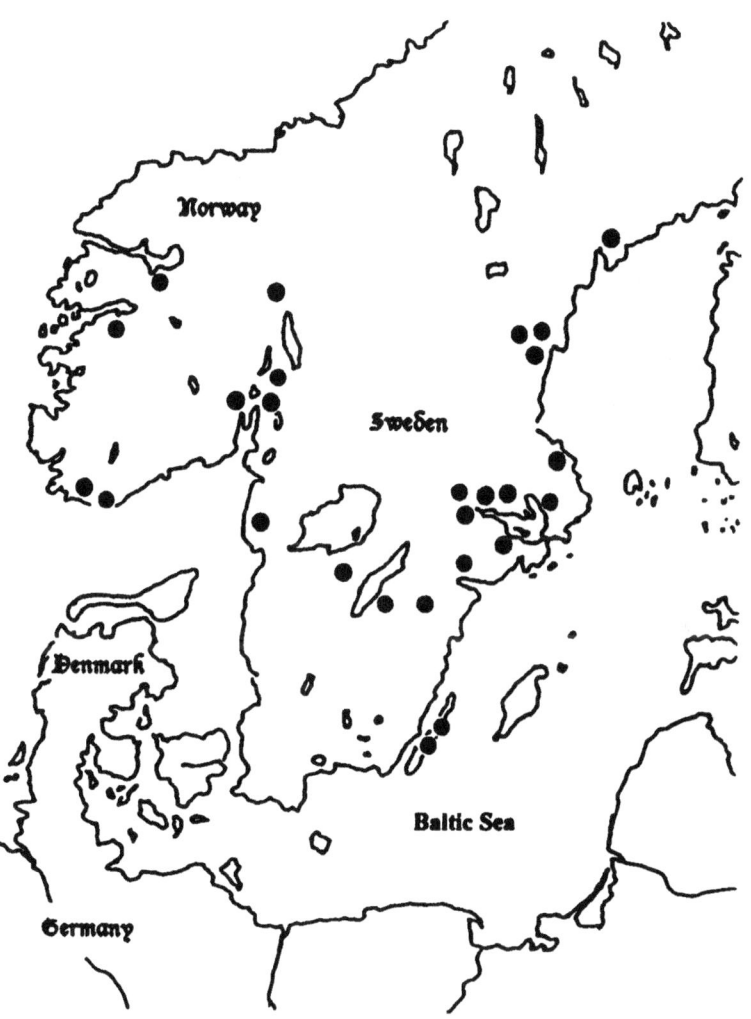

Map V: The Cult Sites of Njörðr

www.ingramcontent.com/pod-product-compliance
Lightning Source LLC
Chambersburg PA
CBHW071007160426
43193CB00012B/1950